A TRENCHERM
TO TH
EASTERN C

COMPILED AND EDITED B...

CONTENTS

Restaurants:

Norfolk	6
Suffolk	30
Cambridgeshire	52
Essex	70
Beds & Herts	90

★ **PRIZE DRAW** 95

Inns:

Norfolk	100
Suffolk	127
Cambridgeshire	144
Essex	151
Herts & Beds	165

Locator maps 186

Index 188

THIS GUIDE IS PRODUCED QUITE INDEPENDENTLY, AND HAS NO CONNECTION WITH ANY COMPANY OR PUBLICATION OF A SIMILAR NAME.

Published by
Bracken Publishing, Bracken House,
199a Holt Road, Cromer, Norfolk NR27 9JN

ISBN 1 871614 26 0

Printed by Broadgate Printers, Aylsham, Norfolk.
March 1997

IMPORTANT

Please note:-

1. Dishes listed are examples only. Menus change frequently, so they will not necessarily be available at all times.

2. Prices, where quoted, may change during the currency of this guide. Average a la carte prices are based on a three course meal without wine, unless otherwise stated.

3. Open hours refer to meals only, up until last orders are taken, unless otherwise stated.

4. Every effort is made to ensure accuracy, but inevitably circumstances alter and errors and omissions may occur. Therefore the publisher cannot accept liability for any consequences arising therefrom.

5. Your comments regarding inns and restaurants, whether featured or not, are especially welcome. All letters will be gratefully acknowledged, and correspondents who particularly impress will receive a **free copy** of the next edition.

6. This is a selection: it is not claimed that all the best establishments in the region are featured.

7. A note to proprietors: if your establishment is not featured, please do not be offended! The area covered is very large, and time limited. If you serve good food in pleasant surrounds, and would like to be considered for the next edition, please write and let us know.

FROM THE SAME PUBLISHER...

A5 size, 320 Pages of text

£11.95 from leading bookshops, or by mail order direct from publisher (see page one for address). Add £1.55 postage and packing = £13.50

RESTAURANTS

RISTORANTE LA VILLETTA
14 High Street, Heacham. Tel: (01485) 570928

Hours: 12 to 2pm (2:30 Suns) Tues - Sat, 7 to 10pm weekdays; 6 to 11pm Sats.
Credit cards: Mastercard, Visa.
Price guide: a la carte £16, lunch from £5. Sun lunch set price £8.95 & £9.95 (2 & 3 courses).

Examples from menu (revised seasonally): *local cockles sauteed in red wine with chives & parsley; vegetable tartlet in tomato sauce; pastas. Fillets of lemon sole poached in white wine with prawn, cucumber & cream sauce; breast of chicken stuffed with paté & wrapped in puff pastry; escalope of veal with peppers, mushrooms, garlic & tomato sauce; vegetable roast. Apple pie; bread & butter pudding; treacle sponge; luxury Italian ice creams. Trad. Sun. roasts with fish alternative & full a la carte.*

Building on early success (the visitors' book is full of enthusiastic remarks), Carl (front of house) and Deborah (chef) Godfrey are ever eager to please and continue to offer exceptional value. If you just fancy a pasta and glass of wine, that's fine, but you will be tempted by an extensive menu and wine list with a distinct Italian flavour, but now including a selection of English and New World wines, again at very fair prices. Guests are encouraged to linger, Italian-style; the newly extended conservatory is an ideal place in which to do so. For something different look out for theme nights, such as Fish, or the quarterly Ladies' Evenings - a chance to socialise and see a demonstration or two. The no-smoking restaurant is cool and elegant, plushly carpeted, pink and blue linen, flowers on each table, whirring ceiling fans. Watercolours by local artists are for sale. Children welcome. Car park to rear.

FISHES' RESTAURANT
Market Place, Burnham Market. Tel: (01328) 738588

Hours: lunch & dinner (last orders 9:30pm, 9pm in winter) Tues - Sun.
Closed over Christmas and two weeks in January.
Credit cards: Mastercard, Visa, Diners, Amex.
Price guide: a la carte £25, weekday lunch £9.40 & £11.95 (2 & 3 courses).

Examples from menus (revised seasonally): *fresh fish terrine; local oysters live or baked with stilton; crab soup; melon & fresh fruit. Monkfish with mussel & orange sauce; salmon fishcakes with crab sauce; turbot fillet with prawn & parsley sauce; crustacean plate; smoked eel; river trout with almonds & bananas; home-baked ham with smoked chicken. Orange & raisin cheesecake; bread & butter pudding; chocolate & Cointreau mousse; bramley, bramble & plum crumble; tiramisu; home-made ice creams; fresh fruit salad. Mostly British cheeses eg Pencarrig. Children's portions.*

Burnham Market is one of Norfolk's most picturesque villages, and indeed historic: Nelson was born and raised very near here - take away the cars and he would still feel at home today. Another link with the North Sea where he learnt his craft is this perennially popular restaurant, which draws on its bounty in the form of oysters from Brancaster, crabs from Weybourne or Blakeney and much else from King's Lynn. Vegetables come fresh from local market gardeners. Featured regularly in a number of leading national good food guides, it remains nonetheless cheerfully unpretentious, bistro-style, with cork tables and floors, shelves full of books on a multitude of topics, and in summer windows full of wonderful 'Morning Glories.' Live lobsters are kept in a tank out of sight, but the cold display is tempting.

SALMON FUSILI
(from Crown Hotel, Wells)

INGREDIENTS

6ozs salmon, skinned & sliced
12 button mushrooms
½ small onion, chopped
1oz butter
1 good pinch of dried dill
½ fish stock cube
100ml white wine
200ml cream or creme fraiche
100g cooked fusili pasta

METHOD

Melt butter in a sauté/frying pan
Add onions, salmon, mushrooms & cook for 2 or 3 mins
Add wine, dill & stock cube, cook for further 2 mins
Add pasta & cream and cook for further 1 in until hot

Serve with warm rolls or French bread.

THE CROWN HOTEL
The Buttlands, Wells-next-the-Sea. Tel: (01328) 710209, Fax: (01328) 711432

Hours: 12 to 2pm, 7 to 9:15pm daily.
Credit cards: Mastercard, Visa, Amex, Diners.
Price guide: a la carte from £19.50, table d'hote £18; a la carte from £7.50, Sun. lunch from £10.
Accommodation: 1 single, 10 doubles/twins, 4 family. Bargain breaks.

Examples from menus (revised periodically): *moules mariniere; choux pastry gougere with prawns, tomatoes & onions, capped with cheese. Fresh local lobster & seafood; pigeon breasts sauteed with bacon, with cream sauce of wild mushrooms; steak & kidney pie; vegetable tagliatelle in tomato & soy sauce. Chocolate truffle; peach brulée; chocolate & ginger torte. Trad. Sun. roasts.*

"The sort of hotel that tired travellers dream about" - so says the Times newspaper. Who knows, perhaps Horatio Nelson scanned the pages of an earlier edition over breakfast here at The Crown, for it was from this Tudor hotel that he departed in 1793 to join his ship "Agamemnon." Latterly it was Sir Peter Scott, famous ornithologist, who took rest and refreshment beneath the venerable exposed timbers, this coast being a Mecca for "twitchers." The beach, a mile out from the harbour and backed by pinewoods, is magnificent, and the town itself is quaint enough to be still recognisable to Lord Nelson. Proprietor Wilfred Foyers is a distinguished practitioner of the culinary arts, and has won many commendations, including the RAC Blue Ribbon award. The everchanging menus are complemented by a carefully considered wine list presented with an explanatory map. Children welcome in certain areas, dogs also. New Garden Room sun lounge.

RECIPES

VICHYSSOISE WITH SMOKED HADDOCK
(from Morston Hall)

INGREDIENTS

6 leeks (white parts only)	
1½ pints light chicken stock	
2 medium potatoes, peeled and chopped	
2 large fillets of undyed smoked haddock, skinned	
1 pint milk	
½ onion, chopped	
1 bay leaf	
seasoning	
sprigs of thyme	

METHOD

Simmer leeks in chicken stock, cover for 20 mins
Meanwhile, place haddock on roasting tray, cover with onion, milk, thyme & bay leaf
Poach in moderate oven (350f, 175c, gas mark 4) until fish flakes away (c. 20 mins)
Add potato, salt & pepper to leeks & stock and cook until potatoes are soft
Liquidise and put through sieve
Take haddock from oven and pour liquid from it into soup
Flake fish into chunky pieces then place in soup

MORSTON HALL
Morston, nr Blakeney. Tel: (01263) 741041, Fax: (01263) 740419

Hours: 7:30 for 8pm every evening. Sunday lunch.
Credit cards: Mastercard, Visa, Amex.
Price guide: Set dinner £26 (4 courses & coffee), lunch £15 (3 courses).
Accommodation: 6 doubles/twins, all en suite, with TV, direct 'phone, tea & coffee, hair dryer. From £65 pp dinner, bed & b/fast.
Bargain breaks Nov, Dec, March, April 3 nights £185pp incl plus afternoon tea on arrival. Tourist Board Highly Commended.

Examples from menus (changed daily): *vegetable terrine, homemade pasta, roasted red pepper & tomato soup; sole turban with mushroom mousse, wild duck with liver stuffing. Rich chocolate torte, champagne jelly with brandy syllabub.*

"Best Newcomer of the Year 1993" (Caterer & Hotelkeeper); "County Hotel of the Year" in a leading good hotel guide; AA two red stars and rosettes; a much coveted red-letter award from a major French organisation: yet more accolades to add to the many accrued by proprietors Justin Fraser, Galton and Tracy Blackiston since they acquired this 17th-century farmhouse hall in March 1992. Much of their trade is repeat business, which is perhaps the most eloquent testimony of all. Personal service and first class food (Galton is a very experienced chef) are essential ingredients, but the Hall itself is full of charm. Bedrooms are huge and beautifully furnished, and the two lounges and restaurant are spacious and most comfortably appointed. Fruits, vegetables and herbs are grown in the 3-acre garden, and other local produce is also favoured in the kitchen. Unusually, wine is listed according to grape rather than nationality. Look out for special evenings (eg Guy Fawkes). Private parties welcome. Two dog kennels. Residential cookery courses.

RECIPES

CARIBBEAN PEPPERPOT
(from Pepperpot Restaurant, West Runton)

INGREDIENTS

4 tblsp vegetable oil

2lbs pork tenderloin

2lbs skinless chicken breast

2ozs chopped shallots

2ozs butter

2 tsp English mustard

½ tsp cayenne pepper

2tblsp brown sugar

3ozs tomato puree

1 large green pepper, cut into thin julienne

1lb button mushrooms

1 pint chicken stock

2ozs double cream

8ozs sweet potatoes

16 heart-shaped croutons

chopped parsley

METHOD

Cut pork & chicken into 2" pieces
Saute in oil until lightly browned
Place in earthenware casserole

Sweat the chopped shallots in the butter
Add mustard, cayenne pepper, brown sugar, tomato puree and green pepper
Pour in chicken stock, add mushrooms & simmer for 5 mins
Pour this over the pork & chicken pieces in casserole
Cover and place in moderate oven (200°c, Gas Mark 5)
Cook for 45 mins
Add double cream

Garnish with boiled sweet potatoes, croutons dipped in pepperpot sauce & chopped parsley

Serve immediately

THE PEPPERPOT VILLAGE RESTAURANT
Water Lane, West Runton, nr Sheringham. Tel: (01263) 837578

Hours: 12 - 2pm Tues to Sun, 7 - 10pm Tues to Sat.
Credit cards: Visa, Mastercard, Eurocard, Amex, Diners Club International.
Price guide: a la carte from £18, table d'hote £17.95; set price 3-course lunch £10.50; Sunday lunch £11.95.

Examples from menus (revised 3-4 months): *grilled mussels in garlic sauce; melting pots of salmon & prawns; mushrooms in stilton cheese sauce. Dover sole; baked sea bass with fennel; sea trout with whole grain mustard sauce; lobster thermidor; swordfish; tournedos chasseur; venison in port & redcurrant sauce; daily home-made vegetarian dish. Lemon soufflé; cygnet surprise (meringue swan filled with fresh fruit & cream with raspberry coulis & ice cream). Choice of three Sunday roasts & supreme of salmon in white butter sauce.*

Royalty and other dignitaries have enjoyed the cooking of Ron Gattlin; during his 34 years with the RAF he was chef to Chief of Air Staff and in charge of catering at RAF Staff College, Bracknell. Now we humble civilians can also partake, here at his own beamed and chintzy restaurant quietly situated just off the main coast road, where he and wife Barbara (front of house) have earned a place in local esteem over the past six years or so. With such depth of experience his 'repertoire' is truly comprehensive, but he does show a special flair for fresh vegetables, always interestingly presented, and for diet-busting cakes and pastries. Yet prices remain modest, even by the standards of this parsimonius region! Romantics should note in their diaries that Valentine's Supper, five courses plus nibbles to start and coffee with mints to finish, is all for just £18 currently, and no extra for the candlelight and flowers on each table!

RECIPES

MOHR IN HEMD WITH HOT CHOCOLATE SAUCE

(from Mirabelle Restaurant, West Runton)

INGREDIENTS

100g plain chocolate

50g breadcrumbs

6 egg yoks

6 egg whites

vanilla essence

little butter

100g caster sugar

icing sugar

100g ground hazelnuts

SAUCE:
4 fl ozs double cream

1 dessertspoon honey

vanilla essence

3 - 4 ozs plain chocolate

METHOD

Whip egg yolks with half the caster sugar until frothy
Melt chocolate in saucepan or microwave, add to add mix
Mix hazelnuts & breadcrumbs together, set aside
Whip egg white with rest of caster sugar to stiff 'snow'
Fold all together into egg yolk mix
Grease pudding bowl and dust in icing sugar, fill to approx. 1/4 of mould
Put into bain-marie and bake at 180°c for 25 - 30 mins

SAUCE:
Bring double cream, vanilla essence and honey to boil
Add chocolate (either in small pieces or pre-melted) with cream
Stir well, serve

Dip chocolate pudding onto warm plate
Pour chocolate sauce over
Finish with dollop of whipped cream

RESTAURANTS   NORFOLK

THE MIRABELLE
Station Road, West Runton, Cromer. Tel: (01263) 837396

Hours : open for lunch & dinner (last orders 9:15pm); closed Mondays;
closed Sunday evenings in winter.
Credit cards : Mastercard, Visa, Diners, Amex.
Price guide : a la carte £17.50 - £22.50. Table d'hote £15 - £23.50. Lunch £10.50 - £12.95.
New Bistro - as many courses as you like, pub prices.
Accommodation : self-contained flat (sleeps 2) from £50 per week in winter to £175
in summer; special all-inclusive breaks.

Examples from menus (a la carte revised seasonally, table d'hote daily): *local asparagus; Cromer crab; Hungarian goulash soup; seafood vol-au-vent; mussels. Salmon & sea bass in butter sauce; turbot; Dover sole; lobster mayonnaise/thermidor; calves liver & sweetbreads; Wienerschnitzel; game in season. Creme brulee; Viennoise apple strudel; fresh figs in Marsala; souffle glace Grand Marnier.* **NEW BISTRO:** *chicken Viennoise; steak & kidney pie; lemon sole meuniere; roast duckling with apple sauce; mushroom stroganoff.*

Behind a modest facade lies a large, bustling French restaurant, now in its 24th year under Austrian proprietor Manfred Hollwoger. One of the longest established and most popular in the region, it is a perennial in the national guides. Two set price menus and an a la carte add up to en extensive choice, (local seafood and game the house specialities), but now a **new bistro** has been added, totally informal - eat as many courses as you like, pay no more than in a pub. Even the most conventional dish is cooked and presented in a way that makes it memorable. Portions are very generous; you will not go away disappointed! Many of the wines in a truly splendid list of 350 are available by the glass. Gourmet nights in winter should not be missed - ask for a schedule. Advisable to book ahead in summer and for weekends.

RECIPES

GALANTINE OF PHEASANT WITH CHESTNUTS & COGNAC
(from Yaxham Mill, Yaxham)

INGREDIENTS

1 whole pheasant, boned out, skin intact

2 cloves garlic, crushed

4ozs sausage meat

2 smoked bacon rashers, diced

2ozs chopped onion

2ozs butter

½ pint chicken/game stock

4ozs fresh breadcrumbs

2ozs chopped parsley

red wine

cognac

METHOD

Cook garlic, sausage meat, bacon, onion, butter & stock together to form stuffing
Add parsley & breadcrumbs
Place stuffing in bird, tie with string
Cook in oven (Gas 6) for 35-45 min, basting with onion, red wine & oil
When cooked, reduce cooking juices, add cognac
Slice galantine when cool
Cover with sauce, sprinkle with whole chestnuts
Return to oven for approx. 10 mins, Gas 3
Serve piping hot

YAXHAM MILL FREEHOUSE & RESTAURANT

Norwich Road, Yaxham, nr E. Dereham. Tel: (01362) 693144, Fax: (01362) 858556

Hours: 11:30am to 2:15pm, 7 to 9:45pm daily.
Credit cards: Mastercard, Visa, Switch.
Price guide: a la carte £19; bar meals from £5.95; Sunday lunch £7.50 & £9.50 (2 & 3 courses).
Accommodation: two 1-bed & two 2-bed cottages, self-contained, also available for B & B.

Examples from menus (revised seasonally): *pan-fried haloumi cheese in breadrumbs & sesame seeds with spinach sauce; baked avocado fiiled with crabmeat & covered in peppermint sauce. Roasted red snapper in pink berry sauce; vegetable filo pies; duck breast cooked in kiwi & ginger; many daily specials. Belgian chocolate torte; mandarin & ginger roulade; raspberry charlotte russe.* **Bar:** *steak & kidney pudding with Irish ale; steaks; curry; chilli; deep-fried cod/skate; daily specials eg terrine of pheasant, stilton & mushroom bake. Treacle sponge; bread & butter pudding; summer pudding. Trad. Sun. roasts.*

The dark (but not satanic) mill, built in 1860, stands out like a beacon here in the flat lands at the very centre of Norfolk. The well equipped self-catering (or B & B) cottages next to it make an excellent base from which to explore the county's many wonderful attractions. But since September '96 traffic has been increasingly headed the other way, towards this new restaurant, revitalised by a local duck farmer, assisted by versatile chef Charles Newcombe. Business lunches can be prepared quickly, but good food is best lingered over - in two cottagey dining rooms (one a former chapel) with crisp white linen and fresh flowers, or in the pleasant little bar. The good natured staff welcome children, and there's live music every Thursday evening.

WARM TIMBALE OF RICE PUDDING WITH A DUO OF CHOCOLATES, SERVED WITH A RASPBERRY VINAIGRETTE & FRESH RASPBERRIES

(from Derek Byrne, chef at The Red Lion, Caston)

INGREDIENTS (serves 4)

Rice pudding:
- 1 pint milk
- 2ozs rice (pearl)
- ½ oz butter
- 2ozs sugar
- 1 vanilla pod

Chocolate mousse:
- 3 egg yolks
- 1½ ozs castor sugar
- ½ pint milk
- 2 leaves gelatin (soaked)
- 8ozs melted chocolate (65% cocoa, or Bournville will do)
- ½ pint double cream
- 4ozs white chocolate (for discs)

Raspberry vinaigrette:
- ⅛ pint raspberries, puréed
- 5 fl ozs oil
- 1 fl oz vinegar
- ½ tsp mustard
- 2 - 4ozs sugar

Simply place ingredients in a bowl and whisk until smooth

METHOD

Rice pudding:
Bring milk to boil, add rice & vanilla
Keep on low heat until rice is cooked
Add butter & sugar

Chocolate mousse:
Boil milk; meantime whisk egg yolks & sugar
Add milk to this mix and place on low heat, stirring until it coats back of wooden spoon
Dissolve gelatin into mix, then strain into melted chocolate
Whisk until smooth, allow to cool
When cool, fold in whipped double cream, place in fridge

To make **white chocolate discs**, melt white chocolate over pot of steaming water
Once melted, pour onto a tray covered with baking parchment and spread thinly and evenly - place in fridge
When nearly set, cut into squares of about ½"

THE RED LION

The Green, Caston, nr Watton. Tel: (01953) 488236, Fax: (01953) 483098

Hours: 11:45am to 2pm, 7 to 9pm, Tues - Sat.
Credit cards: Mastercard, Visa.
Price guide: a la carte £22; bar meals from £4.50.

Examples from menus (revised seasonally): *tartelette of goats' cheese with aubergine purée & tomato, onion & sherry marmalade; carpachio of lamb; mousseline de mer. Lasagne of lemon sole; duck bigorade; breast of chicken with savoury lemon & vanilla bavarois surrounded by wild mushroom sauce; timbale of spinach & courgettes. Marquis du chocolat; orange & ginger pudding; tart tatin.*
Bar: *chargrilled ciabata with pan-fried Cajun chicken; warm bap filled with grilled bacon & fresh sliced banana; deep-fried cod fillet in fresh batter; folded omelettes filled with roast peppers & goats' cheese; jacket potatoes; baguettes.*

From outside it looks like an unexceptional, if still appealing, 16th-century flint country pub on a village green, but the many enthusiastic 'thank-yous' logged in the visitors' book indicate there is much more going on here. In fact, since opening early in 1996 under the ownership of Amrit Virdi, the Red Lion has made its name as one of the region's most promising new restaurants. Success has been based on quality and creativity from the kitchen of chef Derek Byrne, accompanied by a fine wine list of over 100 bins. Browse through the menu in a comfy sofa by an open log fire, then into the small, intimate restaurant, tastefully uncluttered, crisp green and white linen. If the needs of the moment are for a simpler, faster meal, bar food is also very original and tasty. Pianist every Saturday evening and occasionally midweek. Upstairs function room. Children welcome. Garden.

RECIPES

THE ULTIMATE BIG BREAKFAST
(from Richard Hughes of No. 24, Wymondham)

INGREDIENTS

1 escalope of naturally smoked haddock

pan fry in a little butter.

New potatoes

smoked bacon

parsley, chives, salt, black pepper, butter

fry together in butter until bacon is crispy and potatoes are nicely browned - finish with the herbs.

450g ripe tomatoes

1 dess. spoon honey

1 dess. spoon balsamic vinegar

1 onion (diced)

basil, salt, pepper

simmer all together until syrupy to make TOMATO KETCHUP

Poached free-range egg

½ cup white wine

1 dess. spoon whipping cream

125g butter

½ teaspoon curry paste

boil wine and cream together, shake in butter and curry paste, to make CURRY BUTTER SAUCE.

ASSEMBLY

Arrange fried potatoes on a plate, add fish, followed by a good spoonful of tomato ketchup, and top with the egg. Surround with curry butter sauce.

NUMBER 24
24 Middleton Street, Wymondham. Tel: (01953) 607750

Hours: lunch Tues - Sat., dinner from Wed - Sat.
Credit cards: Mastercard, Visa.
Price guide: a la carte dinner £18; lunch main course from £4.95.

Examples from menus (revised fortnightly): *seafood minestrone; cured salmon with blinis; seared scallops with lentils & coriander. Salad nicoise; sauté of chicken with wild mushrooms & Madeira; roasted aubergine with peppered pasta. Chocolate brownie with chocolate malt ice cream; rum & raisin pudding with glazed bananas; coconut waffles with rhubarb compote.*

This popular family-run restaurant goes from strength to strength. Working single-handed in the kitchen, chef proprietor Richard Hughes prepares some of the most innovative dishes around, using local produce, consistently cooked and beautifully presented. As well as recognition from the AA and Egon Ronay, recent accolades include the prestigious 'Menu of the Year', previously bestowed on the likes of the Roux brothers, The Dorchester and Le Talbooth. A regular on Radio Norfolk, columnist in the Caterer & Hotel Keeper and a favourite at many cookery shows around the country, Richard's food is definitely putting Norfolk ingredients on the map! A thriving outside catering business, fine wine dinners and very popular monthly cookery demonstrations mean that the many regulars always have something to look forward to - ask to go on mailing list.

RECIPES

KISSEL
(from Brasted's on the Park, Weston Longville)

INGREDIENTS

| 1lb raspberries |
| 1lb blackcurrants |
| 1 tin (or fresh) black cherries |
| 1lb blackberries |
| 1lb redcurrants |
| 1lb strawberries |

or as many of the above as possible

| 1½ pints blackcurrant cordial |
| ¼ pint fruit juice |
| pared rind of orange and the juice |
| 1 large glass red wine |
| 1 tbsp cornflour |

METHOD

Put juice and wine in large pan with rind & juice of orange
Bring to boil
Add cornflour and stir until juices thicken
Remove from heat and add all the fruit
Allow to cool

Serve in a pretty bowl with a small meringue on top and cream alongside

BRASTED'S ON THE PARK
Weston House, Weston Longville. Tel: (01603) 873232

         Hours: : 12 to 2pm, 7 to 9:30pm daily except Sun.evenings.
   Credit cards : Mastercard, Visa.
     Price guide : a la carte dinner £23; table d'hote lunch £13.50; bar snacks from £1.60
Accommodation : planned for 1997.

Examples from menus (revised 2-monthly): *chicken livers with muscatel & sultana sauce in pastry case; seafood terrine with tomato & basil coulis; fresh pear filled with cheese & herb paté with tarragon mayonnaise. Roast sea bass with lemon beurre-blanc & grilled grapefruit; steak & kidney pudding with tarragon suet crust; risotto of wild mushrooms & sun-dried tomatoes. Cherry clafoutis with kirsch custard; ameretto parfait with butterscotch sauce; creamy walnut cheesecake. Trad. Sun. roasts.*

The contrast in surroundings is marked enough, but here in the glorious parkland of Weston Golf Club this new venture bears the distinctive stamp of John Brasted's other, long established restaurant, a few miles to the east in Norwich. Although naturally frequented by golfers, do not imagine that it's all Pringle sweaters and loud check trousers; this is more a restaurant with golf course attached. Parson Woodforde was a visitor to Weston House, and would feel most at home today amongst the warmth, opulence and copious food and wine - chef John Evans from Gwynedd is acclaimed nationally. All rooms are elegantly proportioned - superb for functions of any kind - and the tall windows afford stirring views. Barbecues are planned for a lovely sheltered courtyard, and a discreetly placed marquee copes with overspill.

CHICKEN WITH BASIL
(from Brasted's, Norwich)

INGREDIENTS

4 chicken breasts
2ozs butter
1 clove garlic, finely chopped
1 tbsp pesto sauce (which contains basil and is available from any good deli)
5 fl ozs dry white wine
1 tbsp lemon juice
2 tbsp finely chopped parsley
salt & pepper

METHOD

Thinly slice chicken breasts lengthways so that you have thin strips of meat
Fry the chicken in 1oz of butter until they turn white
Remove from pan and set on one side
In a medium saucepan melt the remaining butter and add garlic, pesto sauce, white wine & lemon juice
Simmer for 4 mins
Add chicken and cook for further 5 mins
Sprinkle with chopped parsley and serve immediately

Suggest serve with deep-fried courgettes and tossed salad.

BRASTED'S
8-10 St. Andrews Hill, Norwich. Tel: (01603) 625949, Fax: (01603) 766445

Hours: : Fri. 12 to 2pm and 7 to 10pm. Sat. 7 to 10pm.
Credit cards : Mastercard, Visa, Diners, Amex.
Price guide : a la carte £24; Club Lunch £8.50, £12.50 & £16 (2,3 & 4 courses).

Examples from menus (revised 2-monthly): *tart of smoked haddock & leek with watercress sauce; Brasted's filo pastry cheese parcels with homemade apple & thyme jelly; quenelles of salmon in lobster sauce. Lowestoft brill in cream, mushroom & prawn sauce; braised lamb shanks with lentils; steak & kidney pudding; breasts of wild duck with Madeira & green peppercorn sauce; casserole of vegetables. Chocolate Marquise on coffee bean sauce (irresistible!); baked apple with apricots, sultanas & almonds on warm rum-scented apricot sauce; hot souffles. Savoury alternatives (a rare treat).*

John Brasted's philosophy, that one should be able to enjoy fine wines at a manageable cost, is borne out by the excellent wine list, very keenly priced for a restaurant of such high standing. The same may be said of the cooking; the Club Lunch represents outstanding value - why not make the most of it while shopping or exploring the interesting streets and alleys here in the historic city centre, by the ancient Bridewell Prison, now a museum. First take drinks in the homely morning room, then into the dining room. The welcoming, comfortable atmosphere is enhanced by draped walls and luxurious armchairs on a polished wood floor with Persian rugs, coupled with first-class service free of undue servility. Dishes featured constantly on an extensive menu include tart of fresh tomatoes, the filo pastry cheese parcels, quenelles of salmon in rich lobster sauce, and two specialities: a wonderul cassoulet and beef Stroganoff. Maximum use of fresh local produce is evident, sympathetically treated by chef Adrian Clarke.

RECIPES

WARM SMOKED SALMON & A TART OF QUAILS' EGGS WITH BEURRE BLANC
(from Adlard's of Norwich)

INGREDIENTS (serves 4)

1lb fillet of smoked salmon (centre section)
6 quails eggs (2 for spares)
4 cooked tarts about 1½ - 2" across, of short crust pastry

SAUCE:
2 big shallots, finely diced
200ml dry white wine
50ml white wine vinegar
1 tbsp double cream
250gm unsalted butter

METHOD

Sauce - reduce first three ingredients until dry (not burnt)
Add double cream, boil up and add hard butter in small amount, each time whisking it in, careful to keep temperature warm to hot - if sauce is too cold or hot it will split - consistency should be creamy
Season and keep warm

Eggs - cook in boiling water for 2mins 15 secs and refresh in cold water
Peel eggs - ideally leave in fridge overnight in water and peel next day
Should be soft-boiled

Cut salmon in ¼" thick pieces (2 per person)

To finish - warm up eggs in near-boiling water for 30 secs
Drain and season
Warm tarts and fill with eggs
Cook salmon in steamer or char-grill plate so it is cooked on outside and warm, but uncooked in middle

Serve

ADLARD'S
79 Upper St. Giles Street, Norwich. Tel: (01603) 633522

Hours: 12:30 to 1:45pm, Tues. - Sat; 7:30 to 10:30pm, Mon. - Sat.
Credit cards: Mastercard, Visa, Amex.
Price guide: set price £31 (3 courses), £34 (4 courses). Priced by the course.
Lunch £13.50 (2 courses), £16.50 (3 courses).

Examples from menus (revised daily): *seized turbot with gratin of Mediterranean vegetables and basil tomato vinaigrette; grilled teal with salsa verde, pinenuts & herb salad; puff pillow of locally picked wild mushrooms with Madeira sauce. Skate with grain mustard butter sauce & fresh tagliatelle; loin of venison with spatzle, bacon & quenelle of horseradish cream & gratin dauphinois; rack of English lamb with tapenade crust, tart of onion confit & glazed baby onions. Mille feuilles of white chocolate & caramelised bananas; summer pudding with lime syllabub.*

"County Restaurant of the Year" in a leading national good food guide and recipient of a Michelin Star, this is one of the region's élite, with a reputation which extends far beyond. David Adlard moved about nine years ago to this 18th-century grade II listed building in a bustling cul-de-sac near the R.C. Cathedral. He learned his craft at The Connaught, London, is known as a determined perfectionist, and has appeared on national TV, but for all the formidable reputation there is no pretentiousness: simple polished beech flooring on three tiers is complemented by striking green wall fabric and original oil paintings, and the atmosphere is relaxed and unstarchy. Prices are also well within reach, and indeed the lunch menus offer very good value for a restaurant of this calibre. Exceptional wine list of 250 bins from all over the world.

THE STOWER GRANGE RESTAURANT WITH ROOMS
School Road, Drayton, Norwich. Tel. (0603) 860210, Fax (0603) 860464

Hours: : 7 to 9:30pm except Suns; Sunday lunch 12:30 to 2:30pm, other lunches by reservation only.
Credit cards : Mastercard, Visa, Diners, Amex..
Price guide : Set price a la carte £19.95 (no obligation to take all three courses); Sun. lunch £12.25 (3 courses).
Accommodation : 2 singles (from £45 incl.), 7 dbls/twins (from £60, 4-poster £75). Special breaks. All rooms en-suite, TV, phone, free tea & coff.

Examples from menus (revised quarterly): *crab-filled field mushrooms in mustard & cheese sauce; Chinese pancakes filled with crispy duck, with plum sauce. Breast of chicken stuffed with mango, wrapped in bacon, served with light Thai curry sauce & fried rice timbale; lobster thermidor; tournedos Rossini; cherry tomato tart filled with herb cream cheese, with tomato salsa. Sticky toffee pudding; apple & blackberry cheesecake. Trad. Sun. roast plus alternatives.*

It is a common misconception that elegant surroundings such as this equate with starchy formality, or that the wallet is in for a hammering. In truth one is paying very little more than in many a pub, for food of a much higher standard than most. You may elect to have just one or two courses; starter with dessert would set you back only about £10. And there is no standing on ceremony! In two acres of very pleasant grounds, this 17th-century rectory also makes an excellent venue for business or private functions (book well ahead for wedding receptions).

SPECIAL OFFER WITH THIS GUIDE: 50% discount on accommodation if dining (min. 2 persons, subject to availability).

THE DOVE RESTAURANT
Wortwell, Harleston (on A143 by-pass). Tel: (01986) 788315

Hours: anytime, but booking required.
Credit cards: Mastercard, Visa.
Price guide: a la carte £15 to £25, Sun. lunch £8.50
Accommodation: 3 doubles/twins (2 en suite), £32 dble, £17.50 sngle, B & B.
Tourist Board 2 Crowns Approved.

Examples from menus (revised seasonally): *seafood pancake; melon with curried prawns. Own-recipe venison pie; ragout fruits de mer; scampi Provencal; coquilles St. Jacques; chicken supreme; own-recipe steak & kidney pie; trout; steaks. Crepe maison (pancake filled with raspberries, or orange or lemon, and pastry cream); meringue Chantilly; syllabub; chocolate eclair.*

Simple country restaurants serving honest home-cooked food are among the best reasons for visiting France. However, one need only travel as far as the A143 by-pass near Wortwell (not the village itself) to experience the same pleasure. Chef Patron John Oberhoffer, recipient of the Cordon Culinaire award and the Association Culinaire Francais de Londres winner's medal, is a distinguished practitioner of the art of French country cooking. With wife Pat he has over the last 18 years established the Dove as a restaurant respected not just for good food but for the unpretentious manner in which it is presented, and at very reasonable prices. The wine list is mostly French, with some German, but special requests are met when possible. They are also pleased to cater for private parties up to 30, and offer a good breakfast after a comfortable night in one of the refurbished bedrooms - you are well placed here in the lovely Waveney Valley for business or pleasure. A 'Dove' has stood on this acre of ground, bordering a stream, since around the time of the French Revolution.

RECIPES

LOWESTOFT KIPPER & WHISKY PATÉ

(from Karen Aldridge, Chef de Partie, Swan Hotel, Southwold, sister hotel to The Cricketers, Reydon)

INGREDIENTS (serves 8 - 10)

5 x kippers

4 x rashers of bacon, sliced into thin strips

2 x onions, sliced

¼ pint cream

½ lb butter

lemon juice

seasoning

2 x large potatoes, peeled and diced small

2 x tots whisky

METHOD

Gently cook potatoes and onions in butter until soft
Oven-bake kippers; remove skin and bones by sieving
Blend kippers, potatoes and onions with cream until smooth
Gradually add melted butter
Fry bacon in a little oil
Fold in bacon, lemon juice, seasoning and whisky
Pour into cling film-lined terrine mould and refrigerate to set

Serve with hot granary toast and horseradish cream

RESTAURANTS   SUFFOLK

THE CRICKETERS
Wangford Road, Reydon, nr Southwold. Tel: (01502) 723603, Fax: (01502) 722194

Hours: 12 to 2pm, 7 to 9pm daily.
Credit cards: Mastercard, Visa, Amex.
Price guide: set price £13.50 (3 courses); bar snacks & meals from £2.50
Accommodation: 9 bedrooms; single £35, dbl £52, family £73.

Examples from menus (revised daily): *home-made cream of asparagus soup; seafood & pasta salad. Poached halibut steak with mushroom & tarragon sauce; roast baby guinea fowl with Madeira sauce; escalope of pork fillet Sicilian; sauteed lambs' kidneys & mushrooms in red wine sauce.* **Bar:** *king prawns in filo pastry with dill mayonnaise; vegetables & pasta baked in creamy cheese sauce topped with toasted almonds; fresh fish; cold meats platter; daily specials. Homemade sweets. Trad. Sun. roasts.*

The Cricketers (formerly The Randolph) has been a centre of rest and recreation since 1892. Recent renovation has clearly enhanced the public rooms, and cricket memorabilia - prints, photographs of local teams, signed bats - adorn the bright yellow walls. The bar and dining room have also been successfully renovated, and above are nine comfortable bedrooms and a light, airy drawing room. Over the past seven years or so Teresa Doy (manageress) has earned a firm 'thumbs up' from local clientele, reflected in an ever-increasing volume of business, drawn back by delicious food (cooked by long serving head chef Kevin Ellis) accompanied by the award-winning Adnams ales and wines. Yet more improvements are in the pipeline. Parties of up to 60 can be accommodated in the hotel, many more in marquees on the vast lawn.

RECIPES

ROAST LOIN OF ENGLISH LAMB, PARMA HAM, SWEET PEPPER MOUSSE, BASIL & TOMATO JUS OLIVE MASH

(from Simon Reynolds, head chef at The Crown, Southwold)

INGREDIENTS

8ozs lamb loin

2 slice parma ham

½ red pepper, cooked and skinned

4 basil leaves

1 plum tomato, skinned and concassed

8fl ozs good lamb jus

salt & pepper

3-4ozs chicken mousse

½oz butter

6ozs olive oil mash

METHOD

Trim all sinew from lamb, season
Seal in a pan and roast until pink - allow to rest
Wrap chicken mousse around the lamb, then pepper, then parma ham
Wrap in clingfilm and steam for 5 - 10 mins, until mousse is cooked
Heat lamb jus and whisk in butter
Add chiffonade of basil, tomato concasse
Adjust seasoning
Using a round cutter put warmed olive mash into shape
Sauce round the mash
Slice lamb carefully and arrange on the mash.

THE CROWN HOTEL
High Street, Southwold. Tel: (01502) 722275, Fax: (01502) 727263

Hours: 12:30 to 1:30pm, 7:30 to 9:30pm, 7 days.
Credit cards: Mastercard, Visa, Amex.
Price guide: set price £21.50; lunch £16.25; bar meals from £2.95 - £12.50.
Accommodation: 2 singles (£43), 8 doubles/twins (£66), 1 family (£89),
all with private facilities.

Examples from restaurant menus (changed daily): *oak-smoked salmon with quails' eggs & lemon butter sauce; baby spinach salad with melted goats' cheese & roasted pine nuts; Thai soup with coconut milk & Chinese egg noodles. Fillet of sea-reared trout filled with smoked haddock mousse; grilled magret of Suffolk duck with spiced lentils, ginger & carrot sauce; provencal pepper & black olive flan with tomato & feta salad. Orange tart with thin dark chocolate sauce; pistachio & almond filo purses; roast plums with fruit syrup & cream cheese topped with toasted almonds.*

Feted regularly by national newspapers and major food guides, The Crown enjoys a celebrity well beyond the region. Managed by Anne Simpson, it is a flagship for owners Adnams, whose brewery is near, and whose award-winning range of ales is available in both bars. Being also an esteemed wine merchant, the wine list is of course exceptional, with nearly 300 vintages, many available by the glass. But it is as much the food (prepared under the leadership of head chef Simon Reynolds) which wins the plaudits. Its popularity means that booking in the restaurant is always advisable. The essence of an 18th-century coaching inn is still much in evidence - antique furniture, old paintings and carved fireplaces - and the individual bedrooms are simple but attractive. Hotel closed one week in January. Limited parking at rear.

THE SWAN HOTEL
Market Place, Southwold. Tel: (01502) 722186, Fax: (01502) 724800

Hours: 12:15 to 1:45pm, 7:00 to 9:30pm, 7 days. Bar meals 12 to 2:30pm (3pm Sats), 7 days. From late Oct. to Easter restaurant open for lunch on Sat. & Sun. only.
Credit cards: Mastercard, Visa, Diners, Amex, Switch.
Price guide: 3 daily set dinner menus: £21, £27.50, £33.
Lunch £13.25 (2 courses), £15.50 (3 courses); Sundays £15.50 & £17.50.
Accommodation: 6 singles (from £40), 37 doubles/twins (from £86), 2 suites (from £145). Midweek winter breaks from £55 pp incl. 3-course dinner with coffee.

Examples from menus (changed daily): *two-pepper bavarois surrounded by dill sauce; smoked Loch Fyne salmon stuffed with smoked fish served with a horseradish cream; chicken liver & prune pate on bed of leaves with Cumberland sauce. Roast local partridge served with a puree of celeriac with rich game jus; fillet of cod glazed with mozarella, served on plum tomato dressed with yellow pepper vinaigrette; rump of lamb simply baked & garnished with polenta, served with black olive, garlic & tomato concasse port sauce. Bread & butter pudding glazed with an orange preserve, served warm with fresh cream; Amaretto & cinnamon cream surrounded by vanilla sauce; mille feuille of sable biscuits layered with cream & fresh raspberries.*

Southwold is one of England's last unspoilt coastal towns, an enchanting throw-back to an age long past, away from the stresses of the modern world. At its heart is this classic 17th-century hotel, remodelled in the 1820's, and the period refinement and elegance has not been lost to more recent modernisations. Like all the public rooms, the dining room is beautifully furnished, and serves as well for a function as a private dinner for two. The smaller informal Trellis Room, overlooking a tiny courtyard, is used as an extension or for private parties. Three fixed price menus offer a very considerable choice ranging from English classics to some highly original eclectic suggestions from chef Chris Coubrough. He very much favours fresh seasonal produce, using home grown herbs and own-baked bread. Simpler but still excellent fare is available in the bar, accompanied by an award winning Adnams ale, or perhaps a wine from the celebrated Adnams range - Wine Merchants of the Year in 1992, 1993 and 1995. Afternoon teas are another timeless tradition well observed. Bedrooms are very well appointed, individually decorated, and have colour televisions, direct telephones and hair-dryers. Whilst every latest facility is there, the management (led by Carole Wilkin) takes pride in the fact that the hotel continues to provide the very best in ambience, friendly courteous service and first class products. Widely acclaimed in the national press and magazines, this hotel not only serves the needs of one looking for a restful haven of peace, but also the tired business person seeking to relax from a stressful day, or hold an informal business meeting without the interruptions of modern office technology and continous noise of telephones.

ICED LEMON PARFAIT
(from Swan Hotel, Southwold)

INGREDIENTS

3 egg yolks

3 egg whites

4ozs caster sugar

½ pint double or whipping cream

4 lemons, zested and squeezed for juice

METHOD

Line terrine mould with clingfilm
Place egg yolks and 2ozs of the sugar into a bowl and whisk until light in colour and thick
Loosely whip the cream and place in fridge
Pour lemon zest and juice into egg yolk mix and stir
Whip the whites and slowly add the other 2ozs of sugar until whites are stiff and peaky
Fold the cream into the egg yolk mix until clear
Then fold egg whites into the mixture carefully so as not to knock too much air out
When mixed, pour into terrine and cover with clingfilm
Freeze for 2 - 3 hours, serve with fruit sauce, fresh berries to decorate

BAKED TRANCHE OF ALDEBURGH BAY COD TOPPED WITH A MONTAGE OF BRADAN ROST, CREAM CHEESE & CONFETTI OF VEGETABLES

(from David Smith MCFA of Swan Hotel, Southwold)

INGREDIENTS (serves 2)

2 x 3-4ozs fillets of Aldeburgh Bay cod

3ozs Loch Fyne Bradan Roast

4ozs full fat cream cheese

2 spring onions, finely chopped

2 carrots, peeled and grated

2 courgettes (1 yellow, 1 green)

METHOD

Remove any bones from fish but leave skin on, as this protects fish during cooking
Bake on an oiled tray (with knob of butter, sprinkling of salt and pepper, squeeze of lemon) in hot oven for 6 - 10 mins, until fish is nearly cooked
Mix other ingredients together and spread quite thickly on top of cod fillets
Finish under a hot grill for 2 - 3 mins or until golden brown

Serve onto a light plum tomato & red onion salad and a dill vinaigrette

Bradan Rost is a side of fresh West Highland salmon, which is smoked and then kiln-roasted. Available from Simon Bennett, Slaughden Oyster Co, Aldeburgh, tel. 01728 452554

RECIPES

WARM SALAD OF SMOKED CHICKEN
(from Riverside Restaurant, Woodbridge)

INGREDIENTS (serves 4)

4 smoked chicken breasts, cut into thin slices
1 head of raddichio
1 punnet corn salad
2 heads curly endive
1 head oak leaf lettuce
4tbsp olive oil
2 tbsp chopped shallots
raspberry vinegar as required

METHOD

Wash and cut salad leaves into bite-size pieces
Dry, then toss leaves in raspberry vinegar & 2tbsp olive oil
Place a pile of salad into centre of each of four plates
Heat 2 tbsp of olive oil in frying pan, add shallots, fry gently
Place sliced chicken breasts into frying pan
Toss contents of frying pan over high heat
Pour in several tablespoons of raspberry vinegar
Spoon the warmed slices of chicken onto the salad leaves

Chef Vincent Jeffers recommend this dish is best served with an accompanying dry, crisp white wine

Raspberry vinegar may easily be made by mixing together 1lb raspberries, 3 pints white wine vinegar, sugar to taste, then pouring into bottle. Alternatively, the ingredients may be warmed gently, left to stand for five days, then strained into the bottle.

THE RIVERSIDE RESTAURANT
Quayside, Woodbridge. Tel: (01394) 382587, Fax: (01394) 382656

Hours: lunch lunch 12 to 2:30pm, Dinner 6 to 10:30pm, daily except Sun. evenings.
Credit cards: Mastercard, Visa, Amex.
Price guide: a la carte £15 - £20, dinner & film package £19. Light lunch from £3.95.

Examples from a la carte (revised seasonally): *hot chicken liver salad with mayonnaise; special platter for 2 - generous selection of hot & cold hors d'oeuvres. Half a crispy roast duck cooked Chinese-style & served with orange & ginger sauce; fresh grilled tuna with rosemary & garlic; Scottish salmon in filo pastry with spinach & seaweed in lobster sauce. Celebrated homemade puddings eg hot toffee pudding with cream or ice cream; terrine of three chocolates with noisette sauce; pancake parcel filled with curacao souffle or rich double chocolate & praline mousse.*

The Riverside is part of a unique complex containing the luxurious 288-seater theatre/cinema, one of the leading independents in the country. It is thus able to offer a special three-course Dinner and Film package for only £19, plus the exciting a la carte. The airy garden-style restaurant, flooded with light by day, becomes magical at night by candlelight. Enjoy pre-film/theatre drinks in the atmospheric bar, with its antique theatrical mirror and array of old filmstar photographs, while you choose from the Dinner & Film menu, eating before or after the film of your choice. The friendly staff and culinary skills of Vincent Jeffers (head chef) also make for a night to remember. In summer stroll by the Riverside and discover the delights of the ornate gazebo: ice cream, French crepes, cappuccino or espresso coffee, to enjoy under the continental-style canopy. Whatever your choice, you will find proprietor Stuart Saunders true to his word: "The best is not always the most expensive."

TARAMASALATA

(from The Captain's Table, Woodbridge,)

INGREDIENTS

8ozs brown bread crumbs
8tbsp milk
1 clove garlic
1lb smoked cod roe, chopped
1 pint vegetable oil
juice of one lemon
8tbsp yoghurt (Greek sheep's is best)

METHOD

Blend together bread crumbs, milk and garlic in blender
Add cod roe
Blend thoroughly and slowly add vegetable oil
Add lemon juice
Add yoghurt
Blend again

Often served with hot pitta bread.

THE CAPTAIN'S TABLE SEAFOOD RESTAURANT
3 Quay Street, Woodbridge. Tel: (01394) 383145

Hours: lunch & dinner Tues - Sat; 'bar' meals lunchtime and midweek evenings; closed Sundays & Mondays.
Credit cards: Mastercard, Visa, Diners, Amex, Switch.
Price guide: a la carte £16.50, table d'hote £12.95 (3 courses), snacks from £3.25.

Examples from menus (revised frequently): *profiteroles filled with smoked seafood with coriander sauce; terrine of avocado & smoked turkey; local oysters. Coquillage of local fish & shellfish in cheese & sherry sauce; lemon sole fillets filled with prawns in a seafood & ginger sauce; baked aubergine (filled with courgettes, cashew nuts, tomato & basil topped with cheese); sirloin steak. Grand Marnier choc pot; treacle tart with cream; homemade ice creams. Bar meals and daily blackboard specials.*

"According to wind and tide, fisherman's fancy, farmer's whim and gardener's back" - the caveat on the menu (supplemented by a blackboard) is a clue to the fresh provenance upon which diners have been able to rely for nearly 30 years. That's how long Tony Prentice has been running his ever-popular restaurant in one of the region's most attractive and interesting small towns. Yachtsman will often make their way from the quayside straight to The Captains's Table for further communion with the sea and its bounty, although landlubbers are equally keen. The maritime atmosphere is contrived by the felicitous use of fishing nets, seascapes and nautical oddities, including an old diving helmet. The wine list is large and of seriously high quality (not overpriced). If seafood is not your first choice, the vegetarian and meat alternatives are much more than mere afterthought.

WARM SMOKED HADDOCK MOUSSE WITH CRUNCHY VEGETABLES WITH ORANGE DRESSING

(from Scutchers Bistro, Long Melford)

INGREDIENTS

10ozs undyed smoked haddock

3 eggs

7ozs creme fraiche

cayenne pepper

2 carrots

2 raw beetroots

2 courgettes

3 oranges

1 lemon

¼ pint extra virgin olive oil

METHOD

Skin the haddock and puree in a food processor
Add the eggs, season with cayenne
Add creme fraiche and mix for a few seconds only
Butter eight medium-size ramekins and fill with mixture
Cook in water bath for 40 mins at 170c
Meanwhile, peel carrots and beetroot
Cut all vegetables into matchstick-size pieces
Squeeze the oranges and lemon and mix with olive oil
Te serve, scatter the vegetables on a warm plate, spoon on orange dressing
When mousses are cooked let cool for a few mins
Turn out, placing the mousse in the middles of the plate
Serve at once

SCUTCHERS BISTRO
Westgate Street, Long Melford. Tel: (01787) 310200

Hours: 12 to 2pm, 7 to 9:30pm Tues. - Sat.
Credit cards: Mastercard, Visa, Amex, Switch.
Price guide: a la carte £17.

Examples from menu (revised monthly): *Scutcher's smoked salmon & prawn kedgeree with light curry sauce; tempura-style chicken strips on crispy leaves with chilli dressing; fried halloumi cheese with lime & caper vinaigrette. Tandooried monkfish on tomato & coriander salad; roasted breast of duck with apricot & brandy sauce; sautéd wild mushrooms & asparagus on creamy noodles topped with parmesan. Compote of summer fruits with nutmeg & rice pudding ice cream; rich chocolate marquise with caramel sauce; steamed lemon sponge pudding with lemon curd sauce. Blackboard specials from daily market.*

Twice featured on regional television, lauded annually by the main national guides, Nicholas and Diane Barrett continue to maintain exemplary standards, but in an informal 'bistro' style of cooking and presentation, and at very modest prices. Over 100 wines are listed from all over the world, starting from just £7.90 for house wine, the most expensive being only £26. But before they opened they completely gutted this former pub (The Scutcher's Arms), careful not to lose touch with its ancient origins. Split-level tiled floors, farmhouse furniture, pretty floral wall coverings and curtains, inglenook fireplace and a forest of oak beams make for a refreshingly light and pleasant environment. Equally important, the washrooms are unashamedly luxurious!

RECIPES

AUTUMN PIGEON
(from Sue Woods, of the Old Counting House, Haughley)

INGREDIENTS - serves 4

| 8 pigeon breasts |
| 2 - 3 ozs butter |
| 2 tblsp bramble jelly |
| 2 tblsp apple jelly |
| 4 tblsp red wine |

METHOD

Pan-fry the pigeon breasts in the butter for 5 - 10 mins depending on size - should be pink in middle
Remove breasts from pan and keep warm
To the pan juices add wine and jellies
Boil rapidly to reduce by half
Pour over pigeon breasts to glaze
Garnish with blackberries and apple slices

THE OLD COUNTING HOUSE RESTAURANT
Haughley, nr. Stowmarket IP14 3NR Tel & Fax: (01449) 673617

Hours: from 12 noon Mon - Fri. and from 7:15pm Mon - Sat.
Credit cards: Mastercard, Visa, Diners, Amex.
Price guide: table d'hote lunch £14.25 & £16 (2 & 3 courses & coff.);
dinner £22.50 (4 courses & coff.). Bistro menu starters from £2.95,
main courses from £7.50.

Examples from menus (revised 3-weekly): *mushrooms in vermouth; thinly sliced breast of duck with cherry & cinnamon dressing. Salmon in a paper parcel, with white wine & julienne of vegetables; pork fillet with hazelnut stuffing, with apple & wine sauce; pepper & pine nut slice. Butterscotch tart; creme brulée; chocolate & rum ganache; savoury course eg stilton & walnut toasts.*

The chequered history of this marvellous old building goes back to the 13th century, the original still in tact. Custodians for many years have been Paul and Susan Woods. Susan uses nothing that is not absolutely fresh in her cooking. The set price menu is exceptionally good value for four courses and coffee, and there are six choices of starter and main course, plus a selection of home-made sweets, all served on tables laid with Damask linen, classic cutlery and fine glassware. On the last Friday of each month, theme evenings - German or Greek, for example - are very popular, as are the live Jazz Nights (details on request). Some interesting wines from 'down under' are to be found on a list of over 40. This historic village is profuse with flowers in season, being a regular winner of 'Anglia in Bloom'. It is also distinguished by its medieval street, the finest Motte & Bailey in the region, and a church with only five bells (not the usual six) and leather fire buckets still hanging in the tower. Les Routiers and AA recommended. Easy parking.

RECIPES

CHARGRILLED BREAST OF CHICKEN WITH COUS COUS & A TOMATO DRESSING
(from Six Bells Country Inn, Bardwell)

INGREDIENTS (serves 4)

4 chicken breasts

Marinade:
2 tbsp olive oil
2 tbsp lemon juice
1 pinch cinnamon

8ozs cous cous
1 pinch tumeric
1/2 oz sultanas

Dressing:
4 tbsp olive oil
4 tbsp home-made tomato sauce
sprinkling pinenut kernels
tomato concasse

METHOD

Marinade chicken breasts overnight
Chargrill the breasts
Steam cous cous, then mix in tumeric & sultanas
Season to taste
Mix together ingredients for the dressing and warm gently
Present the cous cous in a timbale with thinly carved chicken breast around and dressing alongside
Garnish with a sprig of mint.

THE SIX BELLS COUNTRY INN
The Green, Bardwell, nr Bury St Edmunds. Tel: (01359) 250820

Hours:	12 to 1:30pm, 7 to 9:15pm, 7 days.
Credit cards:	Mastercard, Visa.
Price guide:	a la carte £16; 3-course Sunday lunch £11; bar meals c. £5.
Accommodation:	7 dbls/twins, 1 family; one with 4-poster, all en-suite, TV, radio, phone, tea & coff; B & B £55-70 per room per night; all-year special breaks eg dinner, B & B 2 nights £75pp.

Examples from menus (revised daily): *black pudding, chargrilled potato & caramelised apple with red onion marmalade; mushroom foccacia; potted shrimps in spicy butter. Fillet of smoked haddock rarebit; steak & kidney casserole with herb dumplings; chicken & bacon mousseline in filo pastry with tomato sauce; mushroom & leek duxelle layered with tomato & mushrooms, baked in puff pastry with orange sauce; stilton pork; tipsy lamb. Luxury bread & butter pudding & 'proper' custard; iced chocolate & Tia Maria parfait; banana vacherin.*

In a wonderfully peaceful spot right in the heart of East Anglia, this warm 16th-century inn is a model rural retreat. The individual cottagey bedrooms, converted from barn and stables, are all at ground level, with views over the unspoilt countryside. Overlooking the garden is a bright new conservatory restaurant, or you may prefer the cosier interior, with inglenook fireplaces and beams that have never seen a spirit level! But food is the chief distinction, mostly prepared by proprietor Richard Salmon, who with wife Carol has earned a regular place in most of the major national guides over the past 10 years. They welcome children if parents are well behaved. Good wine list. Small functions.

THURSTON GRANGE HOTEL & RESTAURANT
Barton Road, Thurston, Bury St Edmunds. Tel: (01359) 231260

Hours: 12 to 2pm, 7 to 10pm (9pm Sundays) daily.
Credit cards: Mastercard, Visa.
Price guide: a la carte £16, Sunday lunch £11.25, bar snacks from £3.75.
Accommodation: 2 sngls (£35-£45), 10 dbls/twins (£55-£65), 1 family; all en-suite, TV, phone, hair-dryer, tea & coff. Special breaks: 2 nights dinner, b & b £75pp.

Examples from menus (revised seasonally): *pork & chicken liver terrine with tangy Cumberland sauce; melon with raspberry coulis; home-cured gravadlax. Cod fillet with herb & breadcrumb crust, served with Pernod-&-dill-flavoured cream sauce; vegetarian fricassee; chicken breast pan-fried & filled with apple, celery, sultana & mango chutney stuffing, served with curried cream sauce & basmati rice. Home-made sweets. Trad. Sun. roasts.*

For three generations a family-run business, this beautifully proportioned mock-Tudor mansion stands in splendid isolation, hidden behind tall trees in two acres of parkland and garden. Aproaching via the long, tree-lined drive, the visitor leaves the madness of the A14 a mile behind, trading it for a saner world of sedate pleasures. The tone is set by the panelled entrance lobby, and a beautiful Adam fireplace graces the dignified restaurant. Two lounge bars look out over a south-facing terrace, from where many a wedding party has spilled onto the large lawn - a wonderful setting for such an occasion. The proprietor is also trained chef and wine buff; he prepares classic Anglo-French dishes at extraordinarily reasonable prices. Ideally placed for the region's attractions and a range of country sports.

NUMBER 9 RESTAURANT
9 Park Lane, Newmarket. Tel: (01638) 667999, Fax: (01638) 669096

Hours: 12:30 to 1:45pm Tues - Fri; 7:30 to 9:30pm Tues -Sat; occasional Sunday lunch by arrangement. Hours extended during racing season, incl. Mons.
Credit cards: Mastercard, Visa, Amex, Switch, Delta, Transmedia.
Price guide: a la carte £21, midweek table d'hote £12.95 & £16.95 (2 & 3 courses); lunch £4.95 & £9.95 (1 & 2 courses).

Examples from menus (revised seasonally): *marinated salmon with deep-fried tiger prawns, with fennel & lemon sauce; chicken & pistachio nut paté with toasted home-made bread; lasagne of asparagus & mushrooms with chervil butter sauce. Fresh fish of the day; braised shank of lamb marinated in rosemary, lemon & mint, with dauphinoise potatoes & red wine sauce; pan-fried duck breast with chilli relish & duck confit. Hot chocolate tart with coffee & vanilla sauces; poached fresh fruits with mascarpone ice cream; banana & toffee creme brulée with hazelnut praline.*

In the unlikely setting of an end-of-terrace house in a side street just off the town centre, this new, zestful restaurant is causing quite a stir. Light, bright and modern, the bold use of primary colours, always risky, works well here. The same spirit guides the cooking; best described as modern British, classic dishes are given a new twist, drawing on influences from Europe and the Orient, and presented like a work of art. After a good lunch, perhaps, cosseted in air-conditioned comfort, one might reflect that one has paid little more than in an average pub. Wines, too, are good value, ranging from £9 to £450, and several of the 200+ bins are available by the glass. Unusually, children are made very welcome. Adjacent is a large, free public carpark.

RECIPES

JUGGED HARE
(from Guy Pidsley, Rosery Country House Hotel, Exning)

INGREDIENTS:

2oz fat or dripping

1 pint (approx.) stock

1 clove garlic

1oz flour

1oz tomato puree

1 hare, jointed - ask butcher

redcurrant jelly

GARNISH:
4ozs fried diced streaky bacon

4ozs button mushrooms

chopped parsley

fried bread (1 slice per person)

MARINADE:
¼ pint oil

8ozs onions

stock

8ozs carrots

sprig thyme

2 bay leaves

4ozs celery

few peppercorns

parsley stalks

½ pint red wine

little salt

METHOD:

Soak hare in marinade for 5 - 6 hours
Drain well in colander
Fry pieces of hare in fat or dripping until brown
Place in thick-bottomed pan, mix in flour, cook out, browning slightly
Mix in tomato puree
Gradually add stock
Add all the juice and vegetables from the marinade
Bring to boil, skim and add crushed clove of garlic
Cover with lid and allow to simmer until tender (easily pierced by sharp knife)
Lift out hare (best with slatted spoon!)
Re-boil sauce, add spoonful of redcurrant jelly and more seasoning if necessary
If thickening required, add arrowroot
Pour through strainer over hare
Sprinkle on garnish, serve with fried bread on which redcurrant jelly may be spread
Recommended vegetables: braised red cabbage & apple, creamed potatoes.

THE ROSERY COUNTRY HOUSE HOTEL
Exning, nr Newmarket. Tel: (01638) 577312, Fax: (01638) 577399

Photograph courtesy Gordon Flanagan

Hours: 12 to 2pm, 7 to 9:30pm, Mon - Sat.
Credit cards: Mastercard, Visa, Diners, Amex.
Price guide: a la carte £16-18, bar lunch £9 (3 courses).
Accommodation: 3 sngls, 8 dbls/twins, 1 suite; all except sngls en-suite; TV, direct phone, tea & coff. £50-60 per room incl. Special breaks by arrangement.

Examples from menus (revised constantly): *marinaded fish salad; creamy almond dip with vegetables. Pan-fried lemon sole with bananas; venison steak with orange & elderflower sauce; chicken breast with black grapes & lemon grass sauce; pan-fried fillet steak with blackcurrants, mango chutney & whisky; herb pancakes filled with vegetables, served with creamy peanut sauce; savoury mushroom, nut & tomato bake; daily specials eg halibut with fennel. Home-made sweets.* **Bar lunches:** *butter bean stroganoff; haggis; grills; jacket potatoes; salads.*

Queen Boadicea held court in Exning. Also larger than life but much more welcoming to strangers, Guy Pidsley is a born entertainer; his warm wit greatly amuses guests clustered round the bar at the end of evening they won't forget. With wife Hazel he has thoroughly enjoyed every minute of their 20 years here, and it shows. They take food and drink very seriously, though; the menu is diverse and interesting enough to appeal to everyone, seafood becoming more of a speciality, and it's astonishingly good value. This extraordinary building is imbued with character and does feel like a home-from-home, a place to unwind. Well suited for conferences and private functions, it is handy for Cambridge as well as Newmarket. Children most welcome. Large garden.

MIDSUMMER HOUSE RESTAURANT
Midsummer Common, Cambridge. Tel: (01223) 369299

Hours: 12 to 1:45pm Tues - Fri; 7 to 10:15pm Tues - Sat; plus Sun. lunch.
Credit cards: Mastercard, Visa, Amex, Switch, JCB.
Price guide: a la carte £30, table d'hote £17 & £23 (2 & 3 courses).

Examples from menus (revised seasonally): *gravadlax of red mullet & deep-fried oysters; tartare of veal & roasted pumpkin; deep-fried goats' cheese provencal. Roasted sea bass & fried ravioli of lobster & artichoke; roasted suckling pig with lemon-scented juices; rump of lamb, polenta with couscous, scented with curry; creamed risotto of ceps & truffle with saladaise potatoes. Cheese mousse of white chocolate; prune & almond tart with Armagnac ice cream; banana cream, pistachio brulée.*

West End sophistication at barely half the price - chef patron (since Sept. '95) Anton Escalara was a top London chef, and has also worked in the best of Europe. His perfectionism and passion for his craft are obvious, his menus daringly innovative, the wine list (over 400 bins!) probably the region's largest - a Michelin Star will surely soon be added to the AA third Rosette and high ratings in the all the main national guides. Anton's flair and personality infuse the remarkable circular conservatory dining room - he even commissioned his own tableware from Italy. Upstairs are two superb private dining rooms, one of which affords panoramic views over the River Cam and Midsummer Common, and has a terrace overlooking the enclosed Victorian garden. All this is yours for a short stroll across the Common, or park in Pretoria Road and walk across the footbridge.

STOCKS RESTAURANT
76/78 High Street, Bottisham, nr Newmarket. Tel: (01223) 811202

Hours: flexible - noon onwards, 7pm onwards, except Mons & Sun evenings.
Credit cards: Mastercard, Visa, Delta, Switch.
Price guide: a la carte £25, midweek table d'hote £18.50, lunch £10 & £14 (2 & 3 courses); 'Pot Luck' (Tues eves) £12.95 (3 courses).

Examples from menus (revised monthly): *mousseline of salmon in pillow of puff pastry with asparagus & maltaise sauce; cream of parsnip soup with hint of curry spices (with fresh cream & coriander). Supreme of pheasant in orange & redcurrant sauce with chestnuts & shallots, served with chestnut gnocchi; fillet of monkfish wrapped in bacon & served on buckwheat pancake with shrimp cream & brandy sauce; potato ravioli filled with wild mushrooms & stilton cheese in mushroom-scented sauce; daily specials. Chocolate bread & butter pudding with rum & clotted cream; warm apple charlotte with sauce anglaise & soft fruits; selection of British cheeses with home-made bread. Trad. Sun. roasts.*

At just six years old Amanda Staveley knew she wanted to be in the restaurant business. This is her second, acquired in October '96, and her conviction is manifest; the interior of this handsome 15th-century house (opp. the church) has been transformed to recover its original character, using the most sumptuous fabrics, fine furnishings and antiques. Yet for all the opulence it remains homely, never intimidating. As well as the main beamed restaurant, there is the delightful Orangery or, for private functions up to 16, the wonderful vaulted Tudor Room, air-conditioned and with phone, copying and fax facilities - a unique venue for a business meeting, available free if dining. And you should, for chef Phil Vincent is very experienced and widely respected. Seafood is his speciality, but there are ample alternatives and, given notice, he will prepare a favourite dish to your requirements.

PAPA POMODORO (TOMATO & BREAD SOUP)
(from The Three Horseshoes, Madingley)

INGREDIENTS - serves 20

10lbs plum tomatoes (do not chop too small)
3lbs tinned plum tomatoes
8 garlic cloves
3 large onions, diced small
1 pint good extra virgin olive oil
2 large bunches basil
2 loaves stale (approx. 2 days old) dense bread

METHOD

Place onion in pan with some olive oil, cook but do not boil
Add garlic & tomatoes, simmer for 30 mins
Add 1.5 pints of water & most of olive oil - bring to the boil
Cut crusts from bread, break into large chunks, place in soup
Add basil leaves
Allow bread to absorb all tomato flavouring before serving
May add a little more olive oil if required
If soup too thick, add extra water
Season to taste

THE THREE HORSESHOES
Madingley, nr Cambridge. Tel: (01954) 210221, Fax: (01954) 212043

Hours: 12 to 2pm, 6:30 to 10pm daily (bar & restaurant).
Credit cards: Mastercard, Visa, Diners, Amex.
Price guide: a la carte £18.

Examples from menus (revised three-weekly): *chargrilled scallops with wilted raddicio, chard & chicory, with 30-year-old balsamic vinegar & chive oil; Tuscan bread soup with tomato, beans, cabbage & olive oil. Grilled skate wing with butter beans, rosemary, spinach & lemon butter; pan-fried duck with duck confit, champ, green cabbage, bacon & lentils with red wine & thyme; twice-baked aubergine & ricotta soufflé; roast haunch of venison with red onion marmalade, fondant potato, leeks, mushrooms & juniper. Sunday lunch: roast sirloin of beef.*

Cambridge is surely the region's most visited city, and the consequent bustle can be quite taxing. But just two miles away is to be found this idyllic retreat, a 17th-century thatched inn surrounded by parkland. Highly rated by nearly all the major national good food and pub guides, it is best described as a quality restaurant, although guests are most welcome to just call in for a drink in the bar. One may dine in the bar or the elegant conservatory overlooking the large garden. Richard Stokes is the chef patron, having trained at the famous George Hotel, Stamford and Flitwick Manor. Managing Director is John Hoskins, a wine expert of national standing, whose aim is to list the 100 most interesting wines to be found. Egon Ronay and the Good Food Guide have judged the choice to be outstanding. The Three Horseshoes flourishes as part of the prestigious quartet which includes the Old Bridge Hotel at Huntingdon, The Pheasant at Keyston and White Hart, Gt Yeldham, and follows the same philosophy of friendly informality.

BACON & POTATO TERRINE

(from Fen House, Littleport)

INGREDIENTS

1lb potatoes

1oz butter

2 med. onions, sliced

3ozs streaky bacon, diced

1 clove garlic, crushed

7 fl ozs double cream

4 egg yolks

6ozs thin streaky bacon

METHOD

Peel potatoes and cook in salted water until soft
Drain and slice
Heat the butter in frying pan and cook onions slowly for about 10 mins, stirring frequently
Add diced bacon and garlic and fry over medium heat for three mins
Add cream and boil for one minute
Transfer to a bowl and cool
Mix in yolks and season

Line a 1½ pint loaf terrine with the thin bacon
Build up the filling in layers with the potatoes and cream mixture
Cover with foil or greaseproof paper and bake 'au bain marie' in pre-heated oven at 180°c/350°f (gas mark 4) for about one hour
Remove from oven and press down top of terrine with a weight to help compress the filling
Cool overnight

Remove from the mould and slice into portions
Lay on a plate and re-heat gently in the microwave or on a baking tray in the oven (may also be served cold)
Transfer to the serving plate and garnish

The same idea could be used as a filling for a puff pastry patty

THE FEN HOUSE RESTAURANT
2 Lynn Road, Littleport, nr Ely. Tel: (01353) 860645

Hours: 7 to 9pm (last orders), Tues - Sat; Sunday lunch by arrangement.
Credit cards: Mastercard, Visa, Diners.
Price guide: set price a la carte £25.50 (4 courses); lunch by arrangement.

Examples from menus (revised monthly): *puff pastry case filled with shredded skate & watercress with watercress sauce; fillets of smoked haddock with quails' eggs & wild rice. Rack of lamb with garlic fritters & parsley cream; roast saddle of wild rabbit with mustard noodles; excellent vegetarian options. Caramelised roasted pears with honey ice cream; rich chocolate mousse sandwiched between crisp chocolate layers surrounded by raspberry sauce.*

Michelin and other acknowledged arbiters of good taste laud this little 22-seater gem, heartily endorsed by a well established clientele. David and Gaynor Warne have worked hard over 10 years to earn this recognition for their comfortable, elegant 17th-century cottage out in the 'wilds' of Fenland. One may arrive by car, boat or train (the river and station are very near), but can always look forward to a warm reception from Gaynor, and a well considered and balanced menu prepared by David himself (formerly of The Savoy and Buckingham Palace), to be savoured in relaxed surroundings. All is fresh and home-made, even bread and ice cream, and many of the vegetables are organically grown. 50 or so wines appear on a very good, reasonably priced list. Ask to go on the waiting list for membership of the LUNCHEON CLUB (£10 fee); it's very friendly, with lively discussion over a three-course meal and wine.

RECIPES

WILD RABBIT WITH PRUNES, CIDER & MUSTARD
(from The Anchor Inn, Sutton Gault)

INGREDIENTS - serves 4

1 large or 2 small wild (not farmed - important) rabbits, jointed into about 8 pieces
4ozs smoked streaky bacon, cut into 1" pieces
½ pint strong dry Suffolk cider
1 onion, coarsely chopped
groundnut oil for frying
4ozs whole prunes
1 good dessertspoon quality coarse-grain mustard
seasoned flour
small bunch fresh thyme
small sprig rosemary
2 bay leaves

METHOD

Sweat onion in a little oil until transparent
Add bacon, turn up heat and brown
Remove from frying pan, then add little more oil
Season rabbit pieces
Add rabbit to pan, brown lightly on moderate heat until sealed
Turn up heat, replace bacon and onion
Add cider, prunes, mustard & herbs, and enough water to just cover meat
Bring to boil, stirring bottom of pan to scrape crusty bits
Add a little salt and ground pepper
Put in covered casserole dish and bake in medium to slow oven for about 1½ hrs or until tender
Adjust seasoning to taste if necessary

Serve with simple baked potato or crusty bread, and a green vegetable or salad

THE ANCHOR INN
Sutton Gault, Sutton, nr Ely Tel: (01353) 778537, Fax: (01353) 776180

Hours: 12 to 2pm, 7 to 9pm daily.
Credit cards: Mastercard, Visa, Switch, Delta, Amex.
Price guide: a la carte £22, set-price lunch £14.95 (3 courses), lunchtime specials from £5.
Accommodation: 2 dbls/twins, both en suite, sitting room, TV, phone, dryer, tea & coff; TB 3 Crowns Highly Commended, AA QQQQ; from £55 per room; special 3-night winter breaks.

Examples from menus (revised daily): *grilled dates wrapped in bacon on a mild mustard sauce; herring fillets in Madeira marinade. Fresh fillet of salmon with watercress cream; wild rabbit braised in cider with bacon, mustard, prunes & herbs; steak, kidney & Guinness pie; mushroom, herb, red wine & blue cheese pancake. Passion fruit creme brulée with home-made vanilla biscuit; chocolate Bavarian cream with apricot sauce. Good selection of cheeses. Bar (lunchtime only): own-recipe sausages in red wine with garlic mash; wild mushroom omelette; potted duck with crusty bread. Trad. Sun. roasts.*

Les Routiers Inn of the Year; Cambridge Dining Pub of the Year from another major guide; a Rosette from the Consumer's Association; featured on local TV: despite its glorious solitude, this remarkably preserved (the bar is still gaslit) 350-year-old riverside ferry inn is well and truly 'on the map', even if Sutton Gault itself is not (turn off the B1381 just south of Sutton village). Credit is due to proprietor Robin Moore, assisted by chef Mark Corcoran; their everchanging menus are supplemented by monthly Gourmet Nights on Tuesdays in winter, and there's occasional wine tasting (ask to go on mailing list). Spectacular sunsets and views from bedroom windows. Small function room.

CASSEROLED BRITISH LAMB WITH STILTON DUMPLINGS
(from The Bell Inn, Stilton)

INGREDIENTS

3lbs British lamb, diced	
tbsp sunflower oil	
1lb onions, diced	
1lb shallots, peeled	
1 tbsp English mustard	
2ozs plain flour	
2 pints lamb stock	
1 pint medium sweet cider	
1 bouqet garni	
salt & black pepper	
5 large carrots, sliced	
2 old potatoes, diced	
10 baby sweetcorn, halved (optional)	
5 courgettes, sliced (optional)	

FOR THE DUMPLINGS

½ loaf white bread, diced
5ozs self raising flour
1 packet chives, chopped
4ozs suet
8ozs grated Stilton cheese
½ pint milk
2 x size 3 eggs

METHOD

Heat oil in large ovenproof casserole
Add diced onions & whole shallots, sweat without colour
Add diced lamb, cook until browned, then add mustard
Stir in flour to make a roux
Cook out for 2 - 3 mins
Gradually stir in stock & cider
Season well an add bouquet garni
Cover and cook in preheated oven for one hour
Add carrots & potatoes to casserole and cook further 15 mins

Meanwhile, prepare dumplings:
Mix together diced bread, flour, chives, suet & Stilton in bowl
Add milk & eggs
Divide mixture into approx. 18 portions
Remove casserole from oven
Stir in sweetcorn and courgettes
Drop dumplings into the liquid, cover casserole & cook for further 20 mins
Cook until dumplings are firm but light, ensuring vegetables are cooked and meat is tender

THE BELL INN HOTEL & RESTAURANT
Great North Road, Stilton. Tel: (01733) 241066, Fax: (01733) 245173

Hours: 12 to 2pm, 7 to 9:30pm daily, bar & restaurant.
Credit cards: Visa, Mastercard, Switch.
Price guide: set price a la carte £22.50 (4 courses), table d'hote £15.95, lunch £13.50
Accommodation: 2 sngls, 14 dbls/twins, 1 family, 2 4-posters, all en suite with TV (incl. SKY), phone, haidryers, ironing boards, tea & coff., some with whirlpool baths; singles from £59, doubles/twins from £74; special weekend breaks.

Examples from menus (revised weekly): *salmon & scallop timbale with tomato & coriander sauce; stilton filo baskets. Escalope of venison filled with chicken & chestnut forcemeat on cream & mushroom sauce garnished with truffle; lamb reforme; panache Cherburg (fresh fish gently steamed, coated with cognac & lobster sauce, with Dublin Bay prawn). Sweets from pastry kitchen; stilton & plum bread. BAR: Normandy soup; cajun prawns; steaks; Bell beef pie; baguettes.*

This is one of England's great (and oldest) historic coaching inns, but now that the old A1 has been by-passed it enjoys the tranquility of a country retreat. The 16th-century stonework and timbers have witnessed many a famous face: Dick Turpin, Cromwell, Lord Byron, Clark Gable and Joe Louis amongst them, not forgetting Cooper Thornhill, an 18th-century landlord who first popularised Stilton as one of the world's noblest cheeses. Modern amenities and comforts have been blended skilfully with ancient character: bedrooms are of a luxury undreamt of by earlier travellers, likewise the first class cuisine, which has won accolades from Egon Ronay and other major guides, and the ACE Hotel of the Year 1995 Award. EATB 4 Crowns Highly commended. Excellent facilities for conferences, meetings, wedding receptions etc.

THE CHERRY HOUSE RESTAURANT

125 Church Street, Werrington Village, Peterboro'. Tel: (01733) 571721

Hours: 12 to 2pm Tues - Fri & Sun; 7 to 10pm Tues - Sat.
Credit cards: Mastercard, Visa, Amex.
Price guide: table d'hote £16.95; lunch £12.95 (2 courses), £16.95 (3 courses).

Examples from menus (revised weekly): *venison & pistachio nut sausage on bed of braised red cabbage, cordoned with redcurrant & port jus; filo pastry basket filled with seafood in light Dijon mustard & dill cream sauce. Duo of grilled brill & salmon fillets on bed of leeks with chive butter sauce; medallions of Grasmere Farm pork fillets served with prune & marsala sauce; vegetable & nut strudel served with stilton & port cream sauce. Rich chocolate mousse (spec.); home-made cheesecakes; poached pears with brandysnaps (fruit straight from garden). Trad. Sun. roasts plus alternatives.*

Being chef as well as proprietor, Andrew Corrick can achieve that elusive consistency which is so important. Fresh produce is another key factor, and you don't get much fresher than fruit straight from the garden. Werrington Village (not to be confused with 'new' Werrington) is an island of antiquity in the modern sprawl of Peterborough, and this 400-year-old thatched cottage is its most picturesque building, inside as well as out. A conservatory is used for private parties and there's room for a marquee in the garden - only minutes from Peterborough, The Cherry House makes an excellent meeting place and is popular for business lunches. Prices are remarkably modest for a restaurant of this standing - children under 10 eat at half price.

BENNETT'S RESTAURANT AT THE WHITE HART
Bythorn, nr Huntingdon. Tel: (01832) 710226

Hours: restaurant 12 to 2pm, 7 to 9:30pm except Sun. evenings & Mondays; bar lunch & evening every day except Sat. evenings.
Credit cards: Mastercard, Visa, Switch.
Price guide: a la carte £20.

Examples from menus (revised 5-weekly): *kipper pate; potted pigeon; green herb terrine. Fillet steak & kidney pudding; salmon & scallop parcels with lobster sauce; crispy pancake stuffed with fresh vegetables & pine kernels with tomato & rosemary sauce; half roast Gressingham duck with honey, soy sauce and ginger.* **Bar:** *crispy loin of pork; crispy prawns in batter; game casserole; toasted brie with bacon; sirloin steak; 3-cheese ploughman's; daily specials eg spare ribs, faggots with onions. Homemade sorbets; toasted fresh fruit sabayon. Trad. Sun. roasts.*

Opened on the same day that that the old main road by which it stands was by-passed, The White Hart, more a restaurant than a pub (although drinkers are most welcome), hasn't needed passing trade. Just a mile off the new A14 in a peaceful hamlet, it draws custom from many miles around and has also not gone unnoticed by many of the major national food guides. The fact that it was once three cottages is immediately obvious on entering: stripped-wood floors, low ceilings and a truly magnificent open fireplace engender a rare sense of real atmosphere. A photo from 1910, displayed in the conservatory restaurant (which doubles for functions), shows how little things have changed. Cooking, too, is rooted in the best traditions, yet always imaginative. This food orientation extends to the reading matter thoughtfully provided by Bill and Pam Bennett in the bar. They and the cheerful staff infuse the place with a lively personality. Children welcome. Garden.

DOUBLE-BAKED GOATS' CHEESE SOUFFLÉ WITH APPLE & WALNUT SALAD
(from Pheasant, Keyston)

INGREDIENTS - serves 8

350ml milk	60g strong flour
40g butter	150g goats' cheese
½ tsp mustard	5 egg yolks
5 egg whites	salt & pepper
1 Granny Smith apple,	2 sticks celery
75g walnuts, chopped small	mixed salad
goats' cheese	200g breadcrumbs

METHOD

Make a roux with the butter and flour
Add milk slowly, stirring constantly
When you have added all the milk, add the cheese
Should have thick, paste-like consistency - leave to cool
Butter ramekins with softened butter, coat with breadcrumbs
Add egg yolks to cooled mixture and season with salt, pepper & mustard
Whip egg whites to a soft peak and very gently fold into the cheese mixture
Fill moulds to top (option to place small piece of cheese in middle of each soufflé)
Cook in bain marie in oven for about 20 mins at 160°c

Mix together apple, celery and walnuts, bind with mayonnaise
When soufflés are ready cool them and refrigerate (up to 24hrs)
To reheat, place on baking tray (out of the ramekin) until breadrumbs are lightly toasted and soufflé is doubled in size

To serve: places quenelles of the celery, apple and walnuts around the plate, along with small pieces of cheese. Serve the soufflé on top of the mixed salad

THE PHEASANT
Keyston, nr Huntingdon. Tel: (01832) 710241, Fax: (01832) 710340

Hours: 12 to 2pm, 6:30 to 10pm daily (bar & restaurant).
Credit cards: Mastercard, Visa, Diners, Amex.
Price guide: a la carte £17.50.

Examples from menus (revised fortnightly): *double-baked goats' cheese soufflé with apple & walnut salad; chicken, mushroom & basil sausage with braised lentils & vegetables; fillet of red mullet cured in honey & spices with spiced tomato & coriander sauce. Roast saddle of venison with red cabbage & celeriac purée; baked fillet of cod with herb crust & thyme sauce; char-grilled vegetables with potato & chive salad & red pepper sauce. Citrus lemon tart with creme fraiche; passion fruit delice; rich chocolate marquis with coffee sauce. Trad. Sun. roasts.*

Revered locally and praised by all the main national guides, this picturesque 17th-century thatched inn is a classic of its kind, replete with old timbers and log fires, and overlooking a textbook village green. But a glance at the menu above will confirm this is much more a sophisticated restaurant than a country pub (although drinkers are made welcome). It is as relaxed as any pub, however, in keeping with its stablemates, the Three Horseshoes at Madingley, Old Bridge Hotel in Huntingdon and White Hart, Gt Yeldham. Like them it also boasts an outstanding wine list. Chef patron is Martin Lee, who has worked at the celebrated Le Manoir Aux Quat' Saisons and with Paul Heathcote. Functions up to 30 in restaurant.

SHRIMP DUMPLINGS WITH "JADE" SAUCE

(from Old Bridge Hotel, Huntingdon)

INGREDIENTS

Won ton skins (available from Oriental Stores, Newnham Road, Cambridge)

FILLING:-

1lb raw shrimp, shelved, de-veined and chopped

1 egg white

4ozs shi-itake mushrooms, finely minced

1lb cooked spinach, finely chopped

1.5 tbsp finely chopped ginger

1 tbsp oyster sauce

2 tsp dark sesame oil

0.5 tsp Asian chilli sauce

0.25 tsp sugar

JADE SAUCE:-

1 clove garlic

1 tsp finely grated orange peel

4ozs spinach leaves

2ozs mint leaves

2ozs coriander

8 large basil leaves

1 small spring onion, finely chopped

2 tbsp sherry

2 tbsp white wine vinegar

2 tbsp dark sesame oil

1 tbsp thin soy sauce

2 tsp hoi sin sauce

2 tsp sugar

0.5 tsp Asian chilli sauce

METHOD

To make sauce put all ingredients into blender and purée

Cut won ton skins into circles
Put one teaspoon of the filling into the middle of the skin facing the edges
Seal, then poach in boiling water for 2 mins
Toss the dumplings in the sauce and serve immediately

OLD BRIDGE HOTEL
1 High Street, Huntingdon. Tel: (01480) 452681, Fax: (01480) 411017

Hours: 12 to 2:30pm,
6 to 10:30pm daily
(bar & restaurant).
Credit cards: Mastercard, Visa, Diners, Amex.
Price guide: a la carte £18.
Accommodation: 7 sngls, 19 dbls/twins all en suite, satellite TV, hair dryer, trouser press, complimentary newspaper; rooms from £67.50 to £120 per night; special weekend breaks £67.50 (dinner, b & b).

Examples from menus (revised monthly): *salad of parma ham, tomato, rocket & balsamic vinegar; thin pastry tart with artichokes, olives, aubergine, mozzarella, oregano & pistou; chicken liver parfait with grilled brioche. Pan-fried John Dory with ratatouille and pan-fried pasta; game casserole with rosemary mash potato & roast parsnip; fillet of beef with roast potatoes, mange touts, celeriac puree and bacon, mushroom & red wine sauce. Lunchtime buffet Mon - Fri. Sunday lunch: roast sirloin of beef.*

One of the most respected and best known in the county, this elegant 18th-century hotel (the flagship of the Huntsbridge Group of The Pheasant, Keyston, Three Horseshoes, Madingley and White Hart, Gt Yeldham) is also one of the most opulent. Richly decorated throughout with the finest fabrics (and the bathrooms are luxurious!), it remains nonetheless remarkably 'unstarchy'. The staff are cheerful and courteous, and one may eat what and where one likes. Chef patron Nick Steiger is experienced in top establishments in London and Oxford, while Managing Director John Hoskins is the industry's only "Master of Wine" and winner of Egon Ronay's "Cellar of the Year" for the best wine list in the UK (many available by the glass). The restaurant is clearly no mere appendage, and rates in just about every leading national guide. But the hotel is well situated for an overnight stay, on the banks of the River Ouse and just a short stride from the shops. Cambridge and Grafham water are easily reached. Function room for 30. Live jazz on the terrace first Friday of each month.

RECIPES

BRANDADE OF SMOKED HADDOCK WITH A SALAD OF FINE HARICOTS VERTS & BLACK OLIVES
(from Sheen Mill Hotel, Melbourn)

INGREDIENTS

2 medium-sized jacket potatoes
2 leaves of gelatine
2 fillets undyed smoked haddock, skinned & boned
10 fl ozs milk
2 whites of leek
3 cloves garlic
2 fl ozs double cream per person
salt & pepper
dash lemon juice & brandy
2ozs fine Kenya beans per person
hazelnut oil for dressing
½oz chopped black olives per person
dill & tomato to garnish

METHOD

Cook potatoes in oven until soft; skin and mash until smooth
Soak gelatine in water

Gently poach haddock in milk with leeks, garlic and salt & pepper to taste until cooked (5 - 8 mins)
Strain off fish & leek and blend in food processor; reserve poaching liquid
Squeeze any excess water from gelatine and dissolve it in hot poaching liquor
Mix in fish & leeks
Mix this together with mashed potao and allow to cool before putting in fridge to set
Allowing 2ozs base mix per person, gently fold in 2 fl ozs semi-whipped double cream
Add dash of lemon juice & brandy, adjust seasoning to taste
Gently whisk mixture until you see slight thickening
Refrigerate for one hour

For the salad, blanch fine beans, run under cold water for a few mins to refresh, drain
When dry, dress in hazelnut oil, salt & pepper, and add chopped black olives
Present quenelle of brandade on bed of green beans & olives
Garnish with sprig of dill & tomato concasse

SHEEN MILL HOTEL & RESTAURANT
Station Road, Melbourn. Tel: (01763) 261393, Fax: (01763) 261376

Hours: 12:30 to 2pm, 7:30 to 10pm. Morning coffees. Bar meals in conservatory lunchtimes only.
Credit cards: Mastercard, Visa, Diners, Amex.
Price guide: a la carte from £23, special dinner menu £22.50, lunch from £15.95.
Accommodation: 4 doubles (from £80), 4 singles (£55); all en-suite, TV, direct phone, hair dryer, tea & coff.

Examples from menus (revised seasonally): *braised rabbit faggot with lentils & spring onion; scallop tortelloni with fennel salsa & bayonne ham; rocket & haricot blanc cappuccino. Chump of lamb with spaghetti of leeks & spinach & foie gras cream; confit pig's cheek with morel farce & herb dumpling; escabeche of red snapper with baby vegetables & basil oil; Thai vegetable parcels with herb tagliatelle & walnut pesto. Banana creme brulée with almond praline ice cream; hot mango tart with coconut sorbet & mango coulis; white chocolate tear with vanilla bavarois & biscuit sticks; savouries.*

The individually-decorated bedrooms of this charming 17th-century mill all overlook a glorious canvas, and guests can enjoy the riverside setting from the conservatory perched on the water's edge. Proprietors (for 18 years) Jenny and Carlo Cescutti have built a reputation for fine foods and wine in one of East Anglia's most acclaimed establishments. In the elegant peach, cream and grey restaurant (also with fine views), new chef Tim Lambert insists that all is fresh and home-made - even the delicious chocolates served with coffee - a policy which has secured the coveted AA rosettes and Michelin red 'M'. Theme evenings (eg Jazz, Thai, Seafood) last Friday of each month; regular wine-tastings on Thurs & Fri evenings.

MUSSEL CRESS SOUP
(from Ray Morrison of The Old Hoops, Saffron Walden)

INGREDIENTS

1 quart fresh mussels, cleaned and de-bearded
half-bottle dry white wine
6 shallots, finely chopped
2 sticks celery, finely chopped
whipping cream
1½ozs flour
1½ozs butter
1 large potato, diced small
handful of fresh watercress leaves, chopped
seasoning to taste

METHOD

Place mussels in large pan with wine, shallots & celery
Cook on high heat, stirring occasionally, until shells have opened - discard shells which do not open
Remove from heat, drain liquid and reserve
Remove mussels from shells - discard shells
Double the quantity of liquid with whipping cream
Bring to boil
Thicken with flour & butter worked together into smooth paste
When thickened to soup consistency, add potato
Then add mussels
Simmer for 2 -3 mins
Finish with watercress leaves and season to taste

THE OLD HOOPS
15 King Street, Saffron Walden. Tel: (01799) 522813

Hours: 12 to 2:15pm, 7 to 10pm, Tues. - Sat.
Credit cards: Mastercard, Visa, Diners, Amex.
Price guide: a la carte dinner £20 - 25, lunch £10 - £15; set dinner (Tues - Fri only) £11.95 & £12.95; lunch (all week) £6.95 & £7.95 respectively for 2 & 3 courses plus coff.

Examples from menus (revised frequently): *sopocka (cured loin of pork) with hedgerow bramble jelly; quails eggs on bed of salad with avocado sauce; musselcress soup. Roasted veal chop with sauce of wild mushrooms, cream & mint; breast of chicken stuffed with apricots on port wine sauce; grilled halibut steak with sauce of capers, herbs & cream; pasta filled with ricotta cheese & mushrooms. Cream-filled hot profiteroles with chocolate sauce; lemon posset*

Saffron is the world's most expensive spice, and this pleasant little town was once the centre of trade. Also highly valued but far from expensive, 'The Hoops' can be found right in the middle of the main street, and being on the first floor one can reflect on passing street life whilst digesting the best of fresh food prepared to order. Dating from the 14th century and once a pub, informality still prevails - chef patron Ray Morrison prefers it that way, even though he worked in top West End clubs. With his own style of cooking and attention to detail, he and his family have built an excellent reputation over many years, earning a regular spot in national guides. There's no minimum spend, and the wine list is modestly priced. Booking advisable at weekends.

CHOCOLATE TART
(from White Hart, Gt Yeldham)

INGREDIENTS FOR THE CHOCOLATE

3 egg yolks
2 whole eggs
1.5ozs caster sugar
5ozs butter
7ozs dark chocolate

METHOD

Beat yolks, eggs & sugar until light and fluffy
Melt the chocolate and butter over a double boiler
When just warm, pour onto the egg mixture
Briefly beat together and return to oven at 375°f/190°c/Gas Mark 5 for about five mins
Remove from oven and leave to cool
Serve with thick cream

INGREDIENTS FOR THE SWEET PASTRY

1lb plain flour
8ozs butter
4ozs caster sugar
2ozs "weighed" water
pinch of salt

METHOD

Rub butter into flour until it resembles fine crumbs
Dissolve sugar into COLD water and add to the above mix, bringing slowly together until it forms a ball
Chill for at least 30 mins
Roll out the pastry into a thickness of ¼" and line a 9" flan ring
Chill for 15 mins
Blind bake the flan case for 9-11 mins at 400°f, 200°c, Gas 6
Remove from oven and cool on a cooling rack

THE WHITE HART
Gt Yeldham, nr Halstead. Tel: (01787) 237250, Fax: (01787) 238044

Hours: 12 to 2pm, 6:30 to 9:45pm, daily
Credit cards: Mastercard, Visa, Diners, Amex, Switch.
Price guide: a la carte £18.

Examples of bar/restaurant meals (lunch & evening, 7 days): *chicken liver paté with toasted brioche; Thai mussels with lemon grass, coriander & green chillies; duck confit terrine with haricot bean puree & pickled beetroot. Braised oxtail with mashed potato; tenderloin of pork with red cabbage & apple & Calvados sauce; tagliatelle with pesto sauce, parmesan cheese & tomato & red onion salad. Rich chestnut terrine with chocolate sauce; blackberry & apple crumble with creme fraiche; creme caramel with prunes poached in liqueur muscat. Trad. Sun. roasts.*

Long admired as one of East Anglia's finest Tudor houses, The White Hart is now also marked as amongst its leading pub-cum-restaurants, having recently been acquired by the Huntsbridge Group (Old Bridge, Huntingdon; Pheasant, Keyston; Three Horseshoes, Madingley). Apart from high standards, there's no group 'formula': chef patron Roger Jones has free reign to develop a distinctive style, augmented by regional theme evenings (eg Tuscany, Piedmont). A common feature, though, is an outstanding wine list. One may dine in bar and restaurant; the atmosphere throughout is very special. Small functions and wedding receptions catered for. Large garden.

RISOTTO OF SEA SCALLOPS
(from Le Talbooth, Dedham)

INGREDIENTS

8 large scallops (5 sliced, 3 diced)

11ozs risotto rice

1 shallot, peeled and finely chopped

olive oil

1 pint fish stock, boiling

1 tbsp freshly grated parmesan

1 carrot, peeled and cut into small dice
2 courgettes cut into small dice
(cook in a little butter until al dente)

Salt & freshly ground white pepper

Lemon juice

2ozs double cream, lightly whipped

1/2oz finely chopped chives

few sprigs chervil

METHOD

Sweat the shallot in a tiny amount of olive oil in heavy-bottomed pan for a few mins
Add rice, stir for a few mins
Add 3/4 of boiling stock and cook the rice, adding more stock if required
Keep the rice moving as much as possible to prevent sticking
When rice is ready almost all the liquid should have evaporated and grains should be al dente
Fry scallop slices very quickly in a little olive oil to sear and brown
Stir parmesan cheese, diced vegetables and diced scallop into risotto
Season with salt, pepper & lemon juice
Add cream & chives at very last moment and remove immediately from heat
To serve, place risotto in a bowl and garnish with scallop slices & chervil sprigs

LE TALBOOTH
Gun Hill, Dedham, nr Colchester. Tel: (01206) 323150, Fax: (01206) 322309

Hours:	12 to 2pm, 7 to 9pm daily.
Credit cards:	Mastercard, Visa, Amex, Diners.
Price guide:	a la carte £35; table d'hote £19 & £22 (2 & 3 courses); lunch £15 & £17.50 (2 & 3 courses). 10% service charge.
Accommodation:	10 luxurious suites at nearby Maison Talbooth (transport provided).

Examples from menus (revised two-monthly, table d'hote weekly): *sage-smoked duck with pease pudding, apple & mustard dressing; smooth parfait of foie gras & ducks' liver served with port wine jelly & toasted nut bread; lobster & avocado salad with mango vinaigrette. Pan-fried veal cutlet & sweetbreads, morel cream sauce & straw potoatoes; lightly-roasted troncon of turbot, citrus hollandaise; medallions of venison on turnip & apple rosti, port wine sauce. White chocolate tart "brulée"; ginger marmalade & advocaat syllabub; winter pudding.*

Now in its 45th year (all of them in the hands of the Milsom family), Le Talbooth is amongst England's most widely known and venerated restaurants. It is also one of the most depicted, being a stunning Tudor building beautifully situated on the banks of the River Stour in the heart of Constable Country. To sit out on the terrace under giant parasols is one of the joys of summer. Log fires are winter's compensation, but the marvellous floodlit views can be enjoyed at any time. The menus afford a wide diversity to suit all palates, and prices are not unreasonable for a restaurant of this calibre. Spoil yourself further with a stay at the nearby Maison Talbooth - you won't forget it. You may also like to try the popular seafood restaurant The Pier at Harwich (qv), also owned by the family.

RECIPES

WILD MUSHROOM TERRINE IN A SAVOURY HERB PANCAKE
(from The Pier, Harwich)

INGREDIENTS

PANCAKES:
4ozs plain flour

1 whole egg

½ pint milk

1oz butter

chopped fresh herbs & pinch of salt

MOUSSELINE:
2 x 8oz boneless chicken breast, finely minced

3 egg whites

1 pint whipping cream

pinch mace

salt & ground white pepper

MUSHROOMS: (your choice)
100g dried morels, soaked overnight in salt water, washed several times, pat dry

200g chanterelles

200g Paris pinks

200g shiitake mushrooms

200g oyster mushrooms

All to be washed, dried, tossed individually in olive oil and clarified butter - allow to cool.
Extra herbs for layering terrine - few leaves of sage, chopped chives, dill and parsley.

METHOD - suggest start two days before serving

Line mould with one piece of clingfilm (overhanging)
Make **Pancake batter** (10-12 pancakes):
Place sieved flour, salt & egg in bowl
Slowly beat in milk until a smooth batter is achieved
Heat butter over fast heat until 'nut brown' colour
Whisk into batter and add finely chopped herbs

Line mould with pancakes on top of cling film, overlapping as you go, until mould is covered (allow to overhang)
Make **Mousseline** (ingredients must be ice cold)
Place minced chicken, egg whites & seasonings in food processor and 'blitz' for about one minute
Pour whipping cream while machine is on full speed onto chicken in a steady stream until cream is used - should be dropping consistency (over-processing could result in curdled mix)

Assemble terrine - start with a thin layer of mousseline in lined mould, then alternate with five layers of mushrooms with mousseline & herbs in between - should fill the mould.
Fold overhanging pancakes to cover top; do same with clingfilm
Use 4-fold piece of tinfoil (not lid) to cover

Place finished terrine in roasting tray and half fill with water
Place in oven at 425°f, 210°c, Gas Mark 7 for one hour
Carefully remove from oven, allow to cool, refrigerate overnight
Leave in mould until needed; to remove, lay on side and pull one end of clingfilm - terrine will slide out.
Vinaigrette: ½ pt walnut oil, ½ pt hazelnut oil, 5 fl ozs white wine vinegar, 1 tsp Dijon mustard, salt, pepper, pinch sugar, chopped mixed nuts.

THE PIER RESTAURANT & HOTEL
The Quay, Harwich. Tel: (01255) 241212, Fax: (01255) 551922

Hours: 12 to 2pm, 6 to 9:30pm daily.
Credit cards: Mastercard, Visa, Diners, Amex, Switch, Collect, Delta.
Price guide: a la carte £25, set price dinner £14.50 & £18 (2 & 3 courses); lunch £10.50 & £14 (2 & 3 courses); Sun. lunch £16.50; all subject to 10% service charge; ha'penny Pier Bistro a la carte £11.50.
Accommodation: 6 dbls/twins (2 may be used as family); all en suite, TV, phone, tea & coffee, hair dryer on request; from £50 sngl, £65 dbl; special 2-night break £175 per room (incl. £17.50pp dinner allowance).

Examples from menus (restaurant revised twice-monthly): *gateau of smoked chicken, avocado & soured cream; bisque of local lobster; terrine of spinach & vegetables. Baked fillet of local bass with fresh herb crust on lemon sauce; salmon & dill fish cakes; roasted rack of smoked lamb. Pina Colada cheesecake; almond & coconut tuile basket filled with white chocolate mousse on blackcurrant compote. `Ha'penny Pier Bistro: fish & chips (speciality); fish pie; steaks; savoury veg. crumble.*

You could watch the seafood being landed on the quay on its very short journey to table, via chef/manager (for 18 years) Chris Oakley - one reason why this is one of the most celebrated restaurants in the area. Good, simple and inexpensive snacks may be had in the downstairs bistro. The view is always stunning, especially from the upstairs restaurant, but the nautical decor (a rich marine blue being the theme colour) is also diverting. None of the Victorian grandeur has been lost, and such a strangely quiet location (the town's narrow streets just to the rear) is a marvellous spot for an overnight stay or function (up to 80).

CROFTERS BISTRO & WINE BAR

'Falcon Croft', 25 Maldon Road, Witham. Tel: (01376) 511068

The rear courtyard of Crofters Bistro

Hours: 12 to 2pm, 7 to 10pm daily; bar 11 to 3pm, 6 to 11pm daily.
Credit cards: Visa, Mastercard, Amex.
Price guide: a la carte £12 - £18.
Accommodation: 2 suites, full facilities, TV, phone.

Examples from menus (revised monthly): *platter of Scottish smoked salmon garnished with lemon & parsley; quenelles of honeydew melon garnished with forest fruits. Darnier of salmon grilled with honey & mustard glaze; swordfish steaks with sauce creme; grilled calves' liver & bacon with onion jus; boeuf en croute with madeira sauce; fillet of pork stuffed with apricot, apple & Calvados sauce; steaks; chicken chasseur with rice; vegetarian selection. Home-made desserts.*

If a lottery win has eluded you so far, a few coins invested in the old wishing well of this 18th-century house may pay dividends. If that doesn't work there is ample compensation in the fine wines and culinary flair - in terms both of cooking and presentation - at prices which you needn't be a lottery winner to afford. Over 15 years (itself a rare and telling achievement) proprietor Iva Bird has won wide renown for his epicurean haven just off Witham's main street. The timbered, split-level interior exudes charm, but the 'secret garden' is a delightful discovery for those who venture outside, the more so for being in the town centre. Very comfortable bedrooms, well situated for business or Constable Country. Function room for 35. Parking for 14 plus easy access to Grove Centre car park.

RUSSELLS RESTAURANT
Bell Street, Gt Baddow, nr Chelmsford.   Tel: (01245) 478484, Fax: (01245) 472705

Hours: 12 to 2pm, 7 to 11pm Tues Sun; Mondays by prior arrangement.
Credit cards: Mastercard, Visa, Diners, Amex, Switch.
Price guide: a la carte from £25 (5 courses), table d'hote £16.95 (5 courses, not Sat. evening), lunch £10.95 (3 courses).

Examples from menu (table d'hote revised weekly, a la carte four-monthly): *warm mousse of crab & lobster with dill hollandaise sauce; seared pigeon breast on raspberry vinegar sauce; ravioli filled with spinach & camembert cheese, with piquant tomato sauce. Complimentary sorbet. Fillet of beef with horseradish tartlet on beef jus; roasted haddock with saffron potatoes & white wine chive sauce; pastry case filled with mushrooms, garlic & leeks, on tomato & lentil sauce; flambés. Marzipan ice cream dipped in white chocolate, served in tulip basket; pavlova with toffee cream & pecan nuts; tangy lemon tart. Trad. Sun. roasts.*

For all the passing fads of recent years, the classical Anglo-French restaurant still occupies a prominent place. A skilled exponent, chef Mark Jeans prepares a menu of considerable diversity, among which are numbered many classic favourites, plus vegetarian alternatives, and the last Thursday of every month is Gourmet Night. Guests are invited to say if they prefer food more plainly cooked. The building itself is decidedly English; built in 1372 as a barn, it has a high vaulted ceiling, a plethora of beams and exposed bricks, and a gallery overlooking the main dining area. Proprietors Barry and Juliet Watson came here in June '91 and quickly made their mark. They are especially proud of their excellent 82-strong international wine list. Disabled and conference facilites. Outside catering a speciality.

RECIPES

CALDEIRADA A FRAGATEIRO - FISH CASSEROLE, BARGEE STYLE
(from Alvaro's, Westcliff)

INGREDIENTS

1lb halibut (or any combination of firm white fish), skinned, boned & cut into 1" cubes	1lb potatoes, peeled & thinly sliced
	2 tbsps parsley (incl. stalks), roughly chopped
8 scampi, shelled	1 fresh bayleaf (or 2 dried)
8 scallops (and/or prepared squid), cut into squares	1 cup dry white wine
	seasoning to taste
2 onions, chopped	3 tbsp extra virgin olive oil (pref. Portuguese, but Greek will do)
3 - 4 large ripe tomatoes, peeled & roughly chopped	
	1 small green pepper, de-seeded & thinly sliced (optional)
2 (minimum) large cloves of garlic, crushed	

METHOD

In large pan saute the onion & bayleaf gently in olive oil until softened but not browned
Add garlic and stir
In layers over the onion first place the tomatoes (and optional green pepper), then potatoes, halibut, scampi & scallops (and/or squid)
Sprinkle with parsley & season well
Add wine
Bring to gentle simmer
Cover and simmer for 20 mins, or until potato & fish are just cooked

Serve with fresh crusty bread and side salad

                    Bon Appétit!

ALVARO'S
32 St. Helen's Road, Westcliff-on-Sea. Tel: (01702) 335840

Hours: 12 to 2pm Tues-Fri, 7 to 10:30pm Tues-Sun (11pm Fri & Sat).
Credit cards: Mastercard, Visa, Switch.
Price guide: a la carte from £21.

Examples from menus (revised periodically): *langoustines sautéed in spicy Portuguese piri-piri butter; salted cod (with onion, potato, black olives & egg). Portuguese fish casserole; fillets of sole in light egg batter (pan-fried with banana, Madeira style), beef Alvaro's (large sirloin pan fried in butter with onions, mushrooms, artichokes, & wine, finished with brandy & cream); roast half duckling in port wine sauce; speciality espetadas. Crepes & flambes.*

The Portuguese are, like their oldest allies the English, a maritime nation, but their expertise in cooking with fish puts us to shame. There are no better exponents than Alvaro ('Freddy') Rodrigues and brother Jose (who cooks). Trained in Madeira, they have delighted palates here for over 20 years. Seafood is always to the fore, though steaks, pork, poultry etc. are well featured. The atmosphere and decor are also authentically Portuguese, with the theme of carved and painted cockerels, a legendary national symbol. Naturally, you will find a very fine range of Portuguese wines and old ports, but you may also like to try one of the unusual Portuguese beers. The restaurant is immaculate and service attentive but unobtrusive. Rated highly by both national guides and local people, Alvaro's is just off the main shopping street; from the A127 or A13 take the first left by the lights at Victoria Station onto Hamlet Court Road, then third left - check when you book.

BEEF PAUPIETTES
(from Edelweiss, Leigh-on-Sea)

INGREDIENTS (serves 6)

3lbs top rump beef cut into 6 thin slices
6ozs minced beef
6 slices smoked streaky bacon
6 dill gherkins
2 onions
6 tsp sweet mustard
2tbsp olive oil
a carrot, small leek & parsnip
½ pint beef stock
3 bay leaves & pinch thyme
3 glasses red wine
2 tbsp flour
1 tbsp tomato paste
sprig of parsley
salt & pepper

METHOD

Lay out beef slices and spread on each first mustard, then minced beef, then layer of bacon, then onions
Add to each half a dill gherkin
Roll up meat like Swiss roll and secure at either end with cocktail sticks
Pour olive oil into casserole dish
Place in it the rolled-up meat (paupiettes) and heat over hot flame until browned
Remove from heat, add chopped carrot, leek & parsnip, plus thyme & bay leaves
Sprinkle flour over it, mix in tomato paste
Pour in red wine, top up with stock until covered
Place dish back on heat and bring to boil
Place dish in oven and cook for one hour at 200c or gas mark 6
Remove and strain sauce into pot, season, serve separately
Decorate paupiettes with half gherkins and parsley

Suggest serve with Swiss rosti potato

EDELWEISS SWISS RESTAURANT
1613 London Road, Leigh-on-Sea. Tel: (01702) 711517

Hours: 7 to 10pm, Mon. - Sat; private lunches by arrangement.
Credit cards: Mastercard, Visa, Amex.
Price guide : a la carte £26 - 28 (incl. drinks); 'Schnitzel' menu £12 (Mon - Thurs only).

Examples from menus (specials vary daily): *graubundner fleisch (air-cured beef served on wooden plate with black bread); coquilles d'homard "William Tell" (lobster meat served on shredded apple, lettuce with horseradish mayonnaise, boiled egg); Tournedo Heligoland (fillet steak filled with lobster, roasted with tarragon, in white wine cream sauce); Basler lummelbraten (fillet steak larded with pork fat, roasted & sliced with kidney, served with roast potatoes, celery & cream sauce); vegetarian dishes; flambes; fondues. Sweets & savouries.*

From land-locked mountainous Switzerland to the flat Essex coast - the contrast could hardly be starker, but chef patron Herbert Staudhammer has successfully recreated a little piece of his home country here over the past 17 years. He began in Zurich, garnering further experience from Germany, Paris and at the German Food Centre in Knightsbridge. These influences are brough to bear on his mouthwatering Franco-Germanic menus (only freshest ingredients), though he will be pleased to meet special 'exotic' requests if given sufficient notice - steak & kidney pudding and spotted dick are past examples! The cosy restaurant seats just 40, but there's only one sitting, so one may relax and maybe share a fondue, a most sociable way of eating, accompanied perhaps by one of 14 uncommon Swiss wines.

SEA BASS IN FILO PASTRY WITH SORREL SAUCE

(from David White of The Duke of York, Billericay)

INGREDIENTS

4 x 6ozs portions filleted bass (ensure there are no bones or skin)

1 large onion

2 glasses white wine

½ pint cream

2 sheets filo pastry

4 - 5ozs fresh sorrel

juice of ½ lemon

2ozs butter

METHOD

Preheat oven to 240c (475f) gas mark 8
Melt butter
Lay out filo pastry on board
Brush one sheet with butter, place second sheet over first
Place sea bass onto pastry
Put half the sorrel onto fish
Fold pastry over fish and wrap into parcel
Place onto greased baking tray, brush with remaining butter
Put in oven for 10 - 15 mins

SAUCE:
Reduce wine and cream in pan with diced onions & shredded sorrel
Add lemon juice, salt & pepper to taste

Pour sauce onto plate and place parcel on top. Garnish with lemon wedges.

THE DUKE OF YORK
Southend Road, Billericay (A 129)   Tel: (01277) 651403

Hours: Restaurant 12 to 2pm, 7 to 10pm weekdays; Saturdays 7 to 10pm; Sundays 12 to 2:30pm. Pub hours for bar food as above plus Sat. 12 to 2:15pm. OPEN ALL DAY FOR DRINKS.
Credit cards: Mastercard, Visa, Diners, Amex.
Price guide: a la carte (also in French & German) £20 - £25; table d'hote £16; bar meals from £3.85; Sunday lunch (roast £4.65). Booking advised.

Examples from menus: courgettes provencal; *smoked eel in garlic butter. Fillet of salmon in crab & mussel sauce; local trout Bretonne; strips of veal in tomato & cream sauce; supreme of chicken with bacon & cider sauce; strips of fillet steak in dill & coriander sauce; spinach & tomato roulade with hollandaise sauce; tandoori vegetables on bed of rice; grills; many daily specials. Crepes Suzettes; homemade sweets & gateaux. Trad. Sun. roasts.* **Bar:** *chicken Italienne; home-made pies; fresh skate; Cantonese prawns; fresh pasta dishes.*

Even though the menus are enormous, pride is taken in the freshness of all ingredients. Fish, for example, is delivered daily from the London markets, and some of the sweets and gateaux are made on the premises. Chef proprietor David White specialises in delicious sauces of all kinds, but will cook any dish to customer requirements - flexibility that is the stamp of a family-run business. Those who prefer their food without adornment have a wide choice of grilled meats and fish, and vegetarians have their own separate menu of at least 10 alternatives. Bar meals (except light snacks) may be take in the restaurant. Over 120 wines from all over the world are listed with helpful descriptions, and staff are all well trained in the subject - hence the Routiers Corps d'Elite Award. An outstanding selection of malt whiskies would delight even the most discerning Scot! The antique cash register (in £. s. d.) will stir a little nostalgia.

WHITE CHOCOLATE & ORANGE TORTE
(from Little Hammonds Restaurant, Ingatestone)

INGREDIENTS - serves 12

SPONGE BASE:-
2ozs margarine
2ozs caster sugar
2ozs egg
2ozs self raising flour

MOUSSE FILLING:
1.5lb white couverture chocolate
1 litre whipping cream, whipped to double cream consistency
zest of 2 large oranges, added to cream

METHOD

Cream the margarine and caster sugar for 4 mins on medium speed
Add egg in steady stream, ensuring ingredients mixed together
Add flour on slow mix, taking care not to over-mix
Bake at 170°c for approx. 15 mins

Heat chocolate to 60°c and quickly add to whipped cream
Whisk quickly until clear, or the mix will split

Put sponge base in 8.5" torte ring
Pour in chocolate mix to fill ring
Leave to set

LITTLE HAMMONDS
51 High Street, Ingatestone. Tel: (01277) 353194

Hours: 12 to 2:30pm, 6 to 11pm, 7 days per week (closed Bank Holidays).
Credit cards: Mastercard, Visa, Switch.
Price guide: a la carte £25.50 set price; table d'hote (Sun evening to Sat lunch) £17.95 & £10 (lMon - Sat lunch, excl. Thurs, Fri & Sat evenings); Sun. lunch £12.95.

Examples from menus (revised quarterly, plus daily specials): *ballotine of wild duck with pistachio nuts arranged with French beans, olives & virgin oil dressing; fan of melon with prawns & endives napped with sweet basil dressing. Spinach & blue cheese pie on sautéed pears with tomato sauce; fillet of beef with creamy consomme of celeriac flavoured with veal glace & garnished with dauphinois of celeriac; strips of chicken poached in stock with langoustines, baby vegetables & pink peppercorns, served with sauce of stock, cream & butter. Florentine sablée; flambé desserts.*

Proprietor Stuart Hammond acquired his expertise at various high class hotels and restaurants, and opened here in August 1987. The 'Little' refers to the cottage in which it is housed, which dates from 1558 and is apparently home to a number of ghosts, observed several times by Stuart and staff and the subject of a TV documentary. Undaunted, head chef Kevin Hannaford continues to offer a combination of the best new ideas in cooking, including his own creations, at amazing prices: £10 for a three-course meal is unbeatable value. The restaurant has excellent facilities for a special occasion: the 'Magic Cabaret' seats parties of 10, there is a no-smoking room seating 12 and another private room for 25. Stuart also runs a very professional outside catering service (tel. 352927) for all kinds of events. If the delicious aroma of fresh-baked bread wafts around you, don't look for the paranormal: Stuart's bakehouse is next door!

RECIPES

SPINACH & BLUE CHEESE PIE
(from Little Hammonds, Ingatestone)

INGREDIENTS

PASTRY:
3ozs butter
6ozs flour

- mould together with a little water and pinch of salt

FILLING:
1oz blue cheese
3ozs spinach, blanched
1 shallot, finely chopped, sautéd in butter
salt & pepper to taste

TOMATO & FENNEL SAUCE:
2 shallots, finely diced
2ozs fennel, finely chopped
4ozs rough-chopped tomatoes
½ozs tomato puree
1 star anise
salt & pepper to taste

METHOD

FILLING:
Roll out pastry, press neatly into sides of greaseproof dish
Add shallots to bottom of dish
Press in spinach with the blue cheese on top
Seal a pastry top and brush with egg wash
Cook slowly for 45 mins.

SAUCE:
Sauté shallots & fennel until cooked - without any colour
Add star anise & tomatoes, reduce by half
Season and add purée
Boil until all is cooked
Correct seasoning and pass the sauce
Spread sauce in a circle on a plate and sit pie in the middle

RECIPES

White chocolate & Orange Torte *(see page 86)*

Spinach & Blue Cheese Pie *(see opposite)*

RECIPES

PAPILLOTTE OF RED MULLET SCENTED WITH COURGETTE, LIME & TARRAGON
(from Kirk Ellingham, sous chef Knife & Cleaver, Houghton Conquest)

INGREDIENTS (serves 4)

4 medium-size whole red mullets, or 8 fillets
12 purple shallots, peeled and diced
4 lime leaves, or 4 limes
4 sprigs tarragon
2 courgettes, ends cut off, diced
coarse sea salt
2 sheets greaseproof or tin foil

METHOD

Scale and fillet the fish carefully, as flesh is soft
With tweezers remove the little pin bones that run down the middle
Sprinkle fillets with lime juice and sea salt - leave
Cut greaseproof or foil into large heart shapes large enough to take two fish fillets on one side
Brush each heart shape lightly with butter
Sprinkle with shallots
Place a few leaves of tarragon on one side
Place two fillets on top of this
Sprinkle with diced courgettes & another spoonful of lime juice or a lime leaf
Fold paper in half until the edges meet, then fold tightly all the way round, leaving no gaps
Pre-heat oven to Gas Mark 7, 370°f
Place papillottes on a baking tray for 8 - 10 mins, or until edges are brown
Serve at the table, opening the parcel to release the scents and flavours - fish should be soft and courgettes still well coloured.

THE KNIFE & CLEAVER

Houghton Conquest, nr Bedford. Tel: (01234) 740387, Fax: (01234) 740900

Hours: 12 to 2:30pm, 7 to 9:30pm daily except Sun. evenings.
Credit cards: Mastercard, Visa, Diners, Amex.
Price guide: a la carte £22; table d'hote £17.95 (3 courses); lunch £11.95 (2 courses).
Accommodation: 9 dbls/twins (3 de luxe, 6 stndrd); all en-suite, TV, phone, fridge, hair dryer, tea & coff. RAC 2*; from £45 sngl, £59 dbl; dbl at sngl rate weekends.

Examples from menus (revised monthly): *home-made cannelloni filled with fresh crabmeat & salmon in shellfish soup; goats' cheese paté with walnut & chive topping, with beetroot & red onion marmalade. Loin of lamb stuffed with ginger & spring onion mousse with terryaki gravy; fresh fish eg turbot braised with truffle, herbs & white wine; Mexican-style red pepper & avocado salsa on spiced filo pastry. Own toffee ice cream between layers of banana bread with coffee bean custard; dark chocolate tart with white chocolate sauce.* Bar: *garlicky Toulouse sausages with mashed potatoes & onion gravy; salmon fishcake with fresh spinach, fried potatoes & lemon sauce; lamb & leek pot pie. Trad. Sun. roasts.*

This is one of the county's most widely respected restaurants (recently chosen to cater for the Queen and recipient of AA Rosette), established as such over seven years by David and Pauline Loom, and one of the few where truly fresh fish (a speciality) may be enjoyed. The air-conditioned conservatory dining room (available for functions) is light and airy, and overlooks the flower-bedecked terrace. If eating informally, the bar is also very pleasant, with oak panelling (from nearby Houghton House), low beams and a feature fireplace. Every six weeks on a Friday is a special evening, eg Midsummer live jazz; or try a wine evening, such as Bordeaux, with food to match (ask to go on the mailing list). Spoil yourself with an overnight stay and relax over the papers and a hearty breakfast.

RECIPES

BROWN BREAD ICE CREAM
(from Redcoats Farmhouse Hotel, Redcoats Green)

INGREDIENTS

1 pint double cream

6ozs caster sugar

3 egg yolks

1 dessertspoon liquid glucose (optional but prevents ice cream from being hard)

4ozs brown breadcrumbs

2ozs brown sugar

METHOD

Caramelise the breadcrumbs and sugar by putting them in a moderate oven until browned - leave to cool
Place in liquidiser or food processor and reduce to fine crumb texture
Cream together the eggs and caster sugar until pale creamy colour
Then add glucose (warmed to make it runny)
Add cream and whip up to thick consistency
Fold in breadrumbs and freeze

REDCOATS FARMHOUSE HOTEL
Redcoats Green, nr Hitchin. Tel: (01438) 729500, Fax: (01438) 723322

Hours: 12 to 1:30pm (daily except Sats), 7 to 9pm (daily except Suns). Closed Bank Hols.
Credit cards: Mastercard, Visa, Diners, Amex.
Price guide: a la carte £26; Club Lunch £13 & £15 (2 & 3 courses); Supper Menu from £3.50; Sun. lunch £16.
Accommodation: 1 sngl, 13 dbls/twins; 12 en suite, TV, phone, hair dryer, tea & coff. £70 sngl, £80 dbl, weekend breaks from £100 for 2 nights dinner, b & b.

Examples from menus (revised fortnightly): *fresh scampi tails in garlic butter; home-made rabbit brawn with mustard pickle; roasted tomato salad with pinenuts & olives. Fresh hake cutlet au poivre; fillet steak topped with Guinness & cheddar; grouse served with fried breadrumbs & whisky gravy; casserole of mixed vegetables & pulses on wild rice. Home-made Toblerone & sherry ice cream; peach pudding with walnut & butterscotch sauce; savouries eg angels on horseback, Welsh rarebit. Trad. Sun. roasts.*

"Not so much an hotel, more a way of life" say Peter Butterfield and sister Jackie Gainsford. This 15th-century farmhouse has been in their family since 1916, and is homely in the way that only a family-run business can be, with antiques and paintings, open fireplaces, exposed timbers and an attractive conservatory overlooking the 4-acre garden - a lovely location for a wedding reception (marquee available). Tellingly, chef John Ruffle has worked here for over 16 years, and has earned consistent ratings in the major good food and hotel guides. Now he is bringing on a new 'brigade' of young chefs. Customers become devotees - most of the business is repeat bookings. Tranquil and unspoilt, Redcoats Green is only minutes from the A1 and 35 miles from central London, yet not on the maps - find it off the A602 towards Little Wymondley.

THE LOBSTER TAIL
16 High Street, Gt Offley, nr Hitchin. Tel: (01462) 768391

Hours: 12 to 2pm Tues - Fri, 7 to 9:30pm Mon - Sat.
Credit cards: Mastercard, Visa, Diners, Amex.
Price guide: a la carte £25.

Examples from menu (revised daily according to market): *Scotch smoked salmon; marinated seafood; chef's special paté; tricolore (veg.). Turbot with chablis sauce & prawns; red snapper in spicy Caribbean sauce; seafood thermidor; scallops meuniere; halibut on bed of spinach with mornay sauce; fillet steak chasseur; vegetable stroganoff. Creme Catalan brulée; chocolate parfait; oranges in caramel sauce flavoured with Grand Marnier.*

The very special appeal of fresh seafood is perhaps appreciated all the more by those who live far from the briney. The people of Hertfordshire continue to acclaim this is as one of the very best restaurants of any kind in the county since it opened over eight years ago. The provenance of Billingsgate, Lowestoft and Scotland is chalked up daily on a blackboard and prepared to order (and accompanied by a good wine list). Definitely not on the menu is Osphoremus Gaurami (Delilah to her friends), a large 13-year-old tropical fish in a tank. With intelligent interest she watches over this former 16th-century pub, very cottagey, with soft lighting, candles, flowers, pink and white linen, and a corner alcove for private parties. Gt Offley is a pleasant little village, not far from Knebworth, Whipsnade or Luton Hoo.

Three Meals for two at your Favourite Restaurant to be won

How to enter the Prize Draw

At the top of each page in the inns and pubs section you will see a 'trivia' question about the establishment featured on that page. Some of the clues are a little cryptic, some very straightforward; in most cases it may be fun to find out the answer for yourself, but in a few cases you will need to ask at the bar.

All you have to do is write the answer on the back of a receipt from that same inn or pub and send it to Bracken Publishing at the address shown on page one. You will also need to complete the entry form on page 97 and send that in with your first receipt. After that you may send in as many answers on receipts as you like (remembering to include your name and address each time), but only one per establishment. Each will count as an entry into the draw. So, the more you send in, the better your chance of winning. The prize - a meal for two (plus drinks up to value £20) at any establishment featured in these pages - goes to the first two names drawn.

THERE ARE NO 'TRIVIA' QUESTIONS IN THE HOTELS & RESTAURANTS SECTION, BUT THE READER WHO SUBMITS THE MOST RECEIPTS FROM THIS SECTION WILL WIN A MEAL FOR TWO AT ANY ESTABLISHMENT FEATURED IN THESE PAGES, INCLUDING DRINKS UP THE VALUE OF £20. IN THE EVENT OF A TIE THE ENTRY WITH THE GREATER TOTAL VALUE OF RECEIPTS WINS.

RULES

1. Only receipts from establishments featured in this edition will be accepted.

2. Only one receipt per establishment will qualify.

3. Only one entry form per person will be accepted.

4. Entrants must be aged 18 or over.

5. No photocopies of the entry form or receipts will be accepted (receipts are returnable on request).

6. No entrant may win more than one prize.

7. Meals must be taken before December 31st, 1999, subject to availability.

8. Proprietors and staff of featured inns, pubs, hotels and restaurants may enter but should not submit receipts from their own establishments!

9. Closing date for entries is 31st December, 1998. The draw will take place early in January 1999 and the winners notified as soon as possible. The names of the winners may be obtained by writing to the publisher.

ENTRY FORM FOR PRIZE DRAW

TITLE .... SURNAME ....

FORENAME ....

ADDRESS ....

....

.... POSTCODE ....

TELEPHONE NUMBER..
(WILL ONLY BE USED TO NOTIFY WINNERS)

I BOUGHT MY COPY OF TRENCHERMAN'S GUIDE AT: ....

....

I WOULD LIKE TO RECOMMEND THE FOLLOWING INNS/PUBS/HOTELS/
RESTAURANTS **(CONTINUE OVERLEAF IF NECESSARY)**:-

....

....

....

....

....

....

....

....

....

PLEASE ENTER ME FOR THE PRIZE DRAW AND/OR FREE MEAL
COMPETITION. I HAVE READ AND UNDERSTOOD THE RULES.
I AM OVER 18.

SIGNED.. DATE ....

I WOULD LIKE TO RECOMMEND THE FOLLOWING INNS/PUBS/HOTELS/RESTAURANTS **(CONTINUED FROM PREVIOUS PAGE)**:-

INNS & PUBS

NORFOLK   *Which very special anniversary is celebrated in 1997?*   INNS & PUBS

THE ROSE & CROWN
Old Church Road, Snettisham. Tel: (01485) 541382, Fax: (01485) 543172

Location: near church.
Credit cards: Mastercard, Visa, Switch.
Accommodation: 3 dbls/twins, £30 pp; all en suite, TV, hair dryer, tea & coff.
Oct - March: 2 nights for price of 1 (not Fri & Sat).
Bitters: Adnams, Bass, Woodfordes, Shepherd Neame, guests.
Lagers: Carling, Carling Premier, Tennents Extra.

Examples of bar/restaurant meals (lunch & evening, 7 days): *fresh local mussels in garlic & white wine sauce; home-made country paté; steak & kidney pie (noted); Armenian lamb; steaks; chicken curry; Thai stir-fry; bangers & mash; seared cod on bed of spinach with chive butter sauce; vegetable chilli; fresh-baked baguettes (lunch only); salads, many daily specials. Home-made apple crumble, bread & butter pudding, fresh fruit pavlova, pecan & maple syrup tart. Children's menu. Trad. Sun. roasts £5.95 (1 course).*

This is a country pub which seems to have everything: situated in a lovely corner of the region (near to Sandringham, Norfolk Lavender, Castle Rising and some marvellous beaches); the character of a 14th-century freehouse (old timbers, magnificent open fireplaces, a Public Bar with barrel seats); quality bedrooms at a reasonable price; an outstanding play area with an aviary and rabbits in a pretty, sheltered garden; a large Garden Room (with indoor barbecue), ideal for wedding receptions and other functions. Fresh and dried flowers add their own charm. If this were not enough, food is of a very high order, portions generous and served by friendly staff. Hence the inn has won many awards, and is starred in all the main national guides. A programme of quizzes and entertainment includes live jazz alternate Thursday evenings.

THE GIN TRAP INN
High Street, Ringstead, nr Hunstanton. Tel: (01485) 525264

Location: village centre.
Credit cards: not accepted.
Bitters: Greene King, Charrington, Worthington, Adnams, Toby, Gin Trap Own, Woodfordes, guests.
Lagers: Carling, Tennents, Tennents L.A.

Examples of bar meals (lunch & evening, 7 days): *home-made lasagne; steak & kidney pie (not in brown bowl); steaks; freshly cut ham; chicken Kiev; chicken with leek & stilton; home-made quiches; toad-in-the-hole; scampi; plaice; nut cutlets; daily specials eg h/m mushroom & sherry soup, fresh fish & chips, Home-made bread & butter pudding; treacle pud; fruit crumbles; chocolate brandy cruch cake; sponge puds. Lunchtimes only: jacket potatoes; ploughman's; sandwiches. Children's menu. Trad. Sun. roasts average £5.75.*

"25lb dragon steaks with dwarf beans are available on 30th February, price £400.00" After a few pints of Gin Trap bitter you may feel tempted to tackle this most unlikely entry on the menu, but portions of more conventional fare are in truth generous, though prices somewhat more modest. Since acquiring this 17th-century coaching inn in 1987, Margaret and Brian Harmes have made this one of the area's most popular pubs, a favourite watering hole of ramblers, who are politely requested to remove muddy boots before walking on the monogrammed carpet! Countless gin traps have been cleverly adapted as light fittings, and rural implements of all kinds cover the ceiling. There are two car parks, one of which has stocks where miscreants were once pelted. Why not combine your visit with a look at the adjacent country and sporting art gallery? Walled beer garden. Occasional visits from Morris dancers, and regular entertainment at the piano.

NORFOLK   *What might be thrown away in the window seat?*   INNS & PUBS

THE LIFEBOAT INN
Ship Lane, Thornham, nr Hunstanton. Tel: (01485) 512236, Fax: (01485) 512323

Location:	on a loop off A149 (signposted), overlooking harbour to sea.
Credit cards:	Mastercard, Visa, Switch, Eurocard, Delta.
Accommodation:	13 dbls/twins; all en-suite, TV, phone, hair-dryer, tea & coff. EATB 3 Crowns; from £30pp; special midweek & weekend breaks; most rooms have panoramic views.
Bitters:	Adnams, Woodfordes Wherry, Greene King, guests.
Lagers:	Tennents, Carling. Plus Westons Scrumpy cider.

Examples of bar meals (lunch & evening, 7 days): *venison sausages braised in red wine; brie brulée; Brancaster oysters; crab & ginger filo parcels; roulade of chicken, honey ham & fresh spinach smothered in cheese sauce; Lifeboat fish pie; steaks; ploughman's; sandwiches; daily specials eg roasted guinea fowl in cranberry gravy, grilled whole mackerel coated in lemon butter dressing. Thornham mud pie; hot apple & sultana crumble; lemon curd bread & butter pudding. Children's menu.*

Examples of restaurant meals (as above): *Brancaster mussels (noted); prime fillet of local beef in wild mushroom & cream sauce; roasted peppers stuffed with braised fennel on tomato & herb sauce; supreme of cod brushed with turmeric & sea salt. Chocolate mousse cake with double cream; apple flan Normandy with fresh fruit purée. Trad. Sun. roasts. Afternoon teas.*

Little changed since the 15th century (the Smugglers' Bar is still lit by hanging oil lamps), this former smugglers' alehouse is widely acknowledged as one of the very best on this unique and lovely coast. Proprietors since June '95, Charles and Angie Coker are more than keen to safeguard the very special character of the place. This respect for tradition extends to the kitchen, where "catch of the day" local game and seafood is the house speciality. You may not need a lunch after one of their breakfasts! Guitarist often performs Friday evenings. Children's play area in garden.

THE STIFFKEY RED LION
44 Wells Road, Stiffkey, nr Wells. Tel: (01328) 830552, Fax: (01328) 855983

Location: on A149 coast road, 1 mile from marshes & coastal path.
Credit cards: Visa.
Bitters: Woodfordes (from the barrel), Greene King, guests.
Lagers: two rotating.

Examples of bar meals (lunch & evening, 7 days): *pan-fried liver & bacon with bubble & squeak; steak & kidney pie; roast chicken in tarragon sauce; local crab & mussels; vegetarian dishes; fresh baguettes with various fillings. Sponge puddings; treacle tart; spotted dick; summer pudding; strawberries & cream; local ice cream. Trad. Sun. roast.*

Stiffkey achieved notoriety through its erstwhile vicar, who wanted to save loose women and ended in the jaws of a lion. Being 16th-century, this Red Lion was there long before him, and would seem to have a piano-playing ghost who is given to moving barstools about! It's now the only pub left in one of Norfolk's most picturesque flint villages, but fortunately is one well worth stopping off for. With four open fires, stripped wood and tiled floors, old wooden settles and traditional pub games, the bar is simple and authentic. To the rear are a smart conservatory and dining room. Functions up to 40 are catered for, and outside bars and wedding receptions are gladly arranged. The management is keen on hospitality, and does welcome children. Service is as speedy as possible given that all is fresh and cooked to order (local produce favoured). Terrace overlooks lovely river valley. Large car park.

THE THREE HORSESHOES
Warham, nr Wells-next-Sea. Tel: (01328) 710547

Location: village centre.
Credit cards: under review.
Accommodation: 1 single, 2 doubles (1 en suite), + 2 s/c cottages in N.Creake.
Bitters: Woodfordes, Greene King, guests.
Lagers: Carlsberg.

Examples of bar/dining room meals (lunch & evening, 7 days): *smokie hotpot; game terrine; potted cheese & port; potted smoked fish; cheesy mushroom bake; haddock fillet in cheese sauce; fisherman's pie; rabbit pie; steak & beer pie; cheesy vegetable pie. Spotted dick, steamed syrup sponge, Nelson cake.*

This genuinely unspoilt 18th-century cottage pub will evoke memories of a less frantic age. It's totally 'un-modern', to the extent of a 1940's fruit machine in one corner. Bare floors, open fires, old furniture and gas lighting complete the agreeable illusion. One recent concession to modernity is the brand new toilet block for the disabled. What was the children's room is now a lounge, but families are still welcome, and the garden borders a stream and the village green. Seafood is the house speciality, but the menu includes many meat and vegetarian alternatives, all at very modest prices. Also good value is the accommodation, in a picturebook cottage with roses round the door and working water pump in the garden - an idyllic rural retreat in a timeless flint village.

THE CHEQUERS INN
Front Street, Binham, nr Fakenham. Tel: (01328) 830297

Location: village centre, on B1388 between Wells and Walsingham.
Credit cards: not accepted.
Accommodation: Single £22, dbl £36, family £40 per room incl. TV's, tea & coff. Bathroom adjacent.
Bitters: Adnams Best, Greene King Abbot & IPA, Bass, Toby, guests. Plus Mitchell & Butler's Mild.
Lagers: Carling, Carling Premier, Tennents Extra.

Examples of bar meals (12-2pm daily, 6-9pm Mon-Sat, 6-7pm Suns): *fresh home-made soups; trad. English breakfast; steak & kidney pie; homecooked meats; cod/plaice; whole tail scampi; vegetarian dishes; sandwiches; salads; daily specials eg liver & bacon casserole, pork fillet with apricot, beef & vegetables cooked in ale. Evening specials include fresh local fish and steaks. Trad. Sun. roasts £5.95 (2 courses), 12 - 2pm.*

NB: open 11:30am to 3pm, 5:30pm to 11pm Mon - Sat; 12 to 3pm, 7 to 10:30pm Sundays.

One of Norfolk's finest villages, famed for its ancient priory, Binham is also blessed with one of the county's foremost freehouses, standing in one acre in the village centre. Unusual in that the freehold is held in a charitable trust belonging to the village, the charming 17th-century Chequers has since Jan. '91 been run by current proprietors Brian Pennington and Barbara Garratt. Having gained an enviable reputation for fine food and ales and wines, Brian and Barbara make full use of their culinary skills and the best of fresh local produce to present quality dishes at value-for-money prices. The bar itself oozes character, with its exposed beams and open fires; of special interest is an engraving of the Battle of Portsmouth, during which the Mary Rose sunk. Well behaved children welcome. Large beer garden. No-smoking area. Handy for all the attractions of this lovely area.

NORFOLK — *Name the fools tied in knots* — INNS & PUBS

THE WHITE HORSE HOTEL & FREEHOUSE
4 High Street, Blakeney. Tel: (01263) 740574

Location: village centre.
Credit cards: Mastercard, Visa, Amex.
Accommodation: 2 singles, 4 doubles, 1 twin, 2 family, all en suite bathrooms, TV's, tea & coff; from £30 pp incl; special rates for children and winter breaks.
Bitters: Adnams, Boddingtons, Flowers.
Lagers: Stella Artois, Heineken.

Examples of bar meals (lunch & evening, 7 days): *deep fried herring roes on toast; local whitebait; mussels; fisherman's pie; sirloin steak; local crabs; vegetarian dishes; daily specials eg homemade steak & kidney pudding, tagliatelle with smoked salmon & broccoli sauce, mushroom & stilton pancakes. Spotted dick; treacle tart; bread & butter pudding.*

Examples of restaurant meals (evenings Tues - Sat; booking advised weekends): *char-grilled breast of pigeon with braised turnip & black pudding; poached garden pears with stilton & walnut mousse; grilled fillets of red mullet with spring onion & basil sauce; ballantine of chicken with crab sauce; roast fillet of lamb with sesame & herb crust on red wine sauce. Iced terrine of nougatine with raspberry sauce; grilled pear with hot chocolate sauce & honey & ginger ice cream.*

What a place for a weekend break - the views over the quay from some of the warm, very well appointed bedrooms are superb. The intimate little restaurant (converted from stables) overlooking the attractive walled courtyard has acquired a sterling reputation for good food, accompanied by an excellent wine list. Chef Chris Hyde (formerly of Regatta, Aldeburgh) relies heavily on fresh and mostly local produce, especially seafood. But if your fancy is simply a good pint and maybe a hearty bar meal, this freehouse is also eminently suitable. Residents car park in front of hotel. No dogs.

What is always the time at the dartboard?

THE KING'S ARMS HOTEL FREEHOUSE
Westgate Street, Blakeney. Tel. (01263) 740341

Location: near quayside, west end of village.
Credit cards: Mastercard, Visa, Switch.
Accommodation: 5 dbls/twins, all en-suite, TV; all but one with outstanding views over Blakeney Point; plus self-contained holiday flatlets; £50 per room in summer, £30 winter, incl. breakfast; special breaks & weekly rates.
Bitters: Woodfordes, Webster, Ruddles, Marston's Pedigree, guests.
Lagers: Fosters, Carlsberg, Holsten.

Examples of bar meals (ALL DAY & EVERY DAY; *winter weekdays may vary but food ALWAYS available all day at weekends): home-made pies; seafood pasta; local crabs; mussels; prawns; salads; vegetarian dishes; steaks; fresh fish local trout; salmon; daily specials eg steak & kidney pie, chilli, game pie, filled Yorkshire puds, tuna & pasta bake, spaghetti bolognese. Bread pudding; fruit crumbles; treacle sponge.*

NB OPEN ALL DAY, EVERY DAY

Blakeney would be many people's choice for East Anglia's most picturesque village. Its flint cottages, alleys and courtyards are a delight on the eye, and the views over the marshes provide a lovely backdrop. Just off the quayside (from which there are regular seal trips in season), The King's Arms was once three narrow fishermen's cottages, but is now one of the most popular pubs in the area, recommended by national guides. Licensees Howard and Marjorie Davies left the world of the Black and White Minstrels and My Fair Lady 23 years ago. They welcome children and even dogs if the bar is not full (which in summer it usually is, but there is a garden with swings). Even smokers may appreciate the facility of a no-smoking area in a tasteful new extension, to better enjoy the good food. See if you can spot the 1953 flood tide mark on an inside wall. No piped music or jukebox

NORFOLK *What is forbidden by gracious ordinance of the honourable lords?* INNS & PUBS

THE THREE SWALLOWS
Newgate Green, Cley-next-the-Sea. Tel: (01263) 740526

Location: on village green near church, ½ mile off coast road towards Holt.
Credit cards: not accepted.
Accommodation: 5 dbls/twins, 1 family, all en-suite; £19.50pp in summer, £14 in winter, incl. Eng. breakfast.
Bitters: Greene King, Tetley, Kilkenny.
Lagers: Stella Artois.

Examples of bar meals (lunch & evening, 7 days): *home-made lasagne; steaks; whole prawns in garlic butter; cod; salads; rolls & sandwiches; daily specials eg home-made steak & kidney pie, local mussels in cream sauce, mixed grill, crab salad, Cajun chicken breast, broccoli & stilton quiche. Treacle tart; apple pie; hot chocolate fudge cake. Trad. Sun. roasts.*

It's hard to believe, but Cley was once a large and bustling port. The harbour was directly opposite this 17th-century sailors' inn - the mooring rings can still be seen - but now is a narrow river in open meadows. This peaceful prospect is just one of the pleasures of an unpretentious and homely rural retreat, whose cottage origins are evident in the long, narrow bar, warmed by open coal fires. Dozens of old photos may engage your interest, but of particular note is the ornately carved bar counter. Children are welcome, and the lovely one-acre garden is home to four goats and an aviary. The bedrooms, with their polished wood floors and small sofas, are incredibly good value, especially in such a choice location. The home-made food is also modestly priced.

INNS & PUBS   *What was the exact date of the indenture?*   SUFFOLK

THE BOAR INN
Gt Ryburgh, nr Fakenham. Tel: (01328) 829212

Location: end of village, opp. 13th-century church.
Credit cards: Mastercard, Visa, Connect.
Accommodation: 1 single (£25 per night, £120 per week)), 3 dbls/twins (£45 per night, £190 per week, may be let at single rate), 1 family; all en-suite.
Bitters: Wensum (own brand), Adnams, Greene King, Burtons, Tetley, Kilkenny.
Lagers: Carlsberg, Lowenbrau.

Examples of bar/restaurant meals (lunch & evening, 7 days): *mushroom royale (cooked with stilton & garlic); lasagne; steak & kidney pie; Madras beef curry; salads; steaks; chicken cordon bleu; barbecue lamb cutlets; salmon steak in mushroom & cream sauce; rahmschnitzel; chicken tikka; steaks; prawn creole; daily specials. Meringue glace; fruit crumble; Italian ices.*

With newly refurbished bedrooms, The Boar makes for a marvellous rural retreat in the heart of the county, ideal for an extended visit (and perhaps for a hair-do at the salon on the premises!). But it is principally the food which earns the regular listing in major national guides. All is cooked to order, so allow a little extra time to be served at peak periods. A short stroll to the clear River Wensum, which meanders through a meadow just yards to the rear of the shaded, rose-scented garden (the patio is a sun trap) would fill the time nicely; or take the opportunity to look around this ancient inn - the cosy beamed bar is warmed by an open fire in winter, and the dining room is also very attractive and spacious. Just across the road is an excellent example of the country church for which Norfolk is famed.

NORFOLK *Where did they have a butchers in 1934?* INNS & PUBS

THE CROWN
Colkirk, nr Fakenham. Tel: (01328) 862172

Location: village centre.
Credit cards: Mastercard, Visa.
Bitters: Greene King IPA & Abbot, Rayments Special, Wexford. Plus Mild.
Lagers: Harp, Kronenbourg.

Examples of bar meals (lunch & evening, 7 days): *gratin of mushrooms & prawns; mushroom, ham & leek cheesy bake; cheesy cottage pie; local crab salad; steak & kidney pie; duck liver & armagnac paté; hot Thai chicken; home-made soups; fresh fish of the day; prime Scotch steaks; casseroles; curries; min. 6 veg. choices eg creamy vegetable pancakes; daily specials eg tomato & mozarella salad in basil vinaigrette, tiger prawns in hot oriental sauce, fresh halibut fillet in white wine sauce, fresh battered cod, kidneys in red wine gravy. Homemade hot puddings; gateaux; cheesecake; extensive cheeseboard. Trad. Sun roasts.*

Folk in these parts seem to be unanimous in praise of their local, and it is hard to find fault with such an honest example of the English country pub at its best. The food is fresh and home cooked, the bar and dining room comfortable and pleasant, and the atmosphere congenial. Traditional games like skittles, shove ha'penny, darts and dominoes provide amusement. In winter, warm the extremities with a good hot meal by an open fire; in summer do the same in the sun on the patio or in the beer garden (formerly a bowling green), perhaps with a bottle of wine from a an extensive, personally selected list, all available by the glass - The Crown is noted as one of the top five wine pubs in the country. Pat and Rosemary Whitmore are your amicable hosts, well established here over many years.

Who was the original Earl of Buckinghamshire?

THE BUCKINGHAMSHIRE ARMS
Blickling Road, Blickling, nr Aylsham. Tel: (01263) 732133

Location: at gates of Blickling Hall.
Credit cards: Mastercard, Visa.
Accommodation: 3 dbls/twins; 1 en-suite, all with 4-posters, TV, tea & coff., hair-dryer, trouser press; £60 per room incl., £50 in winter if dining.
Bitters: Reepham, Adnams, guest.
Lagers: Stella Artois, Carlsberg.

Examples from lunch menu (daily): *potato skins with chilli; chicken/steak & kidney pie; lasagne; casseroles; baguettes; daily specials eg mussel soup with lemon grass & ginger, medallions of pork with apple & grain mustard sauce, salmon supreme with sauté potatoes & chive sauce, jalapino pepper stuffed with cream cheese with capiscum dip. Trad. Sun. roasts £6.50 & £7.50 (2 & 3 courses).*

Examples from evening menu (daily except Sundays): *Thai curry; steaks; smoked haddock with cheese sauce; beef/prawn sizzler; chargrilled chicken & bacon melt; grilled whole lemon sole; vegetarian carbonara; real scampi; daily specials. Home-made puddings.*

Given a fresh lease of life by new owners (since June '96) Humble Inns (manager Pip Wilkinson), one of Norfolk's best known and well situated pubs is very much back on the local scene - peak times are very busy. Customers are returning for the modern eclectic cuisine, reasonably priced and served in informal brasserie style. Wine and Gourmet evenings are a regular feature - ask to go on the mailing list. Downstairs has been redecorated, and bedrooms are scheduled for an overhaul, but otherwise this 17th-century inn, built at the same time as the great Hall, remains as it always has been - the original serving hatch can still be seen. Children are welcome and the large sheltered garden has 21 tables.

Which celebrated wartime pilot used to drink here?

THE GOAT INN
Long Road, Skeyton, nr Coltishall. Tel: (01692) 538600

Location: signposted from crossroads at village church.
Credit cards: Mastercard, Visa, Switch, Amex.
Bitters: Adnams, Marston's Pedigree, John Smith, guest.
Lagers: Fosters, Kronenbourg, Carlsberg.

Examples of bar/restaurant meals (lunch & evening, 7 days): *Skeyton hotpot; combos; steaks; steak & ale pie; steak & kidney pudding; lemon chicken; mariner's pie; deep-fried potato skins; vegetable bake; ploughman's; sandwiches; daily specials eg liver & bacon, grilled trout filled with prawns & almonds, pork steaks with apple & brandy sauce, spare ribs with barbecue sauce, NZ green-lipped mussels, mushroom stroganoff. Funky monkey peanut pie; Old Orleans orange pie; spotted dick; jam roly poly. Trad. Sun. roasts.*

What a pleasant discovery to stumble upon in the labyrinth of country lanes (good for walking and cycling) in these parts. Restored and revitalised by Rod and Marian Saunders and family when they took over in February '95, this 16th-century inn is also very attractive inside; light, airy and spotlessly clean, it still has the original timbers, lovely open fires, a barn extension with vaulted ceiling, and eye-catching displays of dried flowers. One may dine anywhere in its three rooms, and functions for up to 20 can be catered for. Children are welcome, and to the rear are seven acres of field with goalposts and play equipment, and sunny terrace with pergola. Good local favourites are the mainstay of the menu; being freshly cooked, there may be a wait of up to 30 mins at peak times. Sure to appear in national guides before long.

What would you get if you asked for one eye?

THE FUR & FEATHER INN
Woodbastwick, nr Norwich. Tel: (01603) 720003

Location: on main road through village.
Credit cards: not accepted.
Bitters: full Woodfordes range.
Lagers: Heineken, Stella Artois.

Examples of bar/restaurant meals (lunch & evening, 7 days): *chicken & mushroom croissant; ham & mushroom tagliatelle; pork spare ribs; Woodforde's pie; Fur & Feather pie (local game in red wine gravy); Woodforde's Yorky; seafood tagliatelle; whole lemon sole; broccoli & cream cheese bake; ½lb burger topped with prawns; veggie burger; canneloni, spinach & ricotto; leek & stilton bake; steaks. Fatal attraction; spotted dick; treacle sponge; lemon meringue.*

NB: restaurant open Tues-Sat evenings, bar food every session.

This being the Brewery Tap, the full range of Woodforde's cask-conditioned ales (available in take-home casks), including more than one national 'champion', is dispensed to eager devotees. It has only a few yards to travel from the brewery next door. But this is no mere drinker's den; cleverly converted by John Marjoram, Jean Skelton and Woodfordes from 19th-century farm cottages in 1992, one of Norfolk's newer pubs quickly become one of its most popular, not just for the beer but for a surprisingly wide choice of traditional homecooked food served in pleasant surroundings. Live entertainment is planned for winter - ask for details. Take time to see the village itself, a throwback to an earlier age, with cottages and a church clustered around a green, and not a car in sight. Lovely Salhouse Broad is also an easy walk.

NORFOLK *In what year did this ferryman's cottage become a pub?* INNS & PUBS

THE FERRY INN
The Green, Stokesby. Tel: (01493) 751096

Location: riverside, near village green.
Credit cards: not accepted.
Bitters: Adnams, Tolly's, guest.
Lagers: Stella Artois, Heineken.

Examples of bar meals (lunch & evening, 7 days): *pork fillets in sweet & sour sauce; chilli; curry; Norfolk garden pies; steaks; lasagne; fresh Cromer crab; natural plaice in lemon butter sauce; trout; Ferryman's lunch; salads; vegetarian lasagne; 4 daily specials. Cheesecake; fruit pies; gateaux. Children's menu. Trad. Sun. roasts.*

Stokesby is one of Broadland's finest: picturesque, tranquil, unspoilt, all the better for being off the beaten track. The river is probably busier than the road in summer, and many of the boats pull in to this eye-catching 18th-century former cottage, right on the water's edge and rated by major national guides. Inside will not disappoint: wooden settles and beams, corner seats and brassware. The cottage origins are most evident in the the large two-tier family lounge, whose concession to the 20th century is a few electronic games in one corner by the entrance. There is a family room, but in kind weather children will want to sit out by the river or head for the play area on the village green. A board on the terrace describes how there was once a ferry across the river, and will provide the answer to the question above!

Who was landlady from 1928 to 1971?

THE FISHERMAN'S RETURN
The Lane, Winterton-on-Sea. Tel: (01493) 393305 / 393631

Location: near village centre and fine sandy beach.
Credit cards: pending.
Accommodation: 3 doubles. £30 single, £45 dbl incl; rooms are quaint with sloping ceilings; tea & coff. facilities;2 bathrooms, 2 sitting rooms with TV.
Bitters: Adnams, Wolf, John Smiths, unusual guests; own micro-brewery planned for 1997.
Lagers: Holsten, Fosters, Kronenbourg. Plus James White & Scrumpy Jack cider.

Examples of bar meals (lunch & evening 7 days): *deep-fried camembert with port jelly; leek & mushroom soup with French bread; ratatouille topped with stilton; medley of salmon & plaice in caper & mushroom sauce; poached monkfish on bed of rice & spinach with mild curry sauce; lamb moussaka; chicken & leek tagliatelle; carbonnade of beef with savoury wild rice; Caribbean pork; fresh salmon provencale; vegetable Madras; aubergine & red kidney bean casserole. Apple & blackberry crumble; lemon & lime cheesecake; double chocolate gateau.*

The windows were once permanently boarded up, as so many bodies were thrown through them when the fishing fleet returned! These days customers usually enter by the door, and find themselves in surprisingly roomy converted 300-year-old fishermen's cottages. To the rear a spacious room for families overlooks a patio and garden with swings and a small menagerie. In winter the open fires broadcast their warm welcome - the winds off the sea are bracing at times. This strange and beautiful coast is a marvellous spot to recharge one's spirits, and for a more prolonged stay there are three charming bedrooms, old fashioned but comfortable. All food is home-cooked to a standard which routinely earns credit from Egon Ronay and other leading guides. Good choice of at least 20 malt whiskies, 13 wines and champagne. Large function room. Dart board.

THE FERRY INN
Ferry Road, Reedham. Tel: (01493) 700429. Fax (01603) 700999

Location: by River Yare, on B1140.
Credit cards: Visa, Mastercard, Switch, Delta, Diners.
Accommodation: adjacent 4-acre caravan & camp site, full facilities.
Bitters: Woodfordes, Adnams, Tetley, Kilkenny.
Lagers: Holsten Export, Tuborg Gold, Carlsberg.

Examples of bar meals (lunch & evening 7 days): *vol-au-vent (chicken in creamy asparagus sauce); poached egg florentine; flaked fillets of smoked trout with horseradish sauce; steak sandwich; curry; lasagne; prawn Newburg; halibut steak with lemon, chervil & chive butter; braised local pheasant; devilled lambs' kidneys; pork fillet stuffed with smoked ham, fresh sage; mozarella, on mustard sauce; charcoal grills; vegetarian choux pastry case; salads; sandwiches; daily specials incl. sweets. Children's menu. Trad. Sun. roasts £5.50 main course.*

The last working chain ferry in East Anglia has been operating since the 16th century, and remarkably is still the only crossing point in over 20 miles. The inn is therefore guaranteed fame of a kind, but the Archers, who run both it and the ferry, make it worth a call on its own merit. Apart from serving good home-made food in clean and pleasant surrounds (one of the two dining rooms - bookable for functions - is no-smoking), they are considerate hosts, offering to make up a bottle for the baby and providing changing facilities in the ladies washroom, for example. Older children are well accommodated in a large sun lounge with arcade machines overlooking the river. From the table and chairs on the bank one can watch the various craft ply the waters. There are moorings and a slipway for trailed boats, and next to the inn a landscaped four-acre caravan and camping site with full facilities (incl. electric hook-ups and free hot water), plus an interesting woodcraft shop. Petits Feathercraft/Theme Park is very near.

INNS & PUBS   *What are the good deeds in the bar?*   NORFOLK

THE KING'S HEAD
Bawburgh, nr Norwich. Tel: (01603) 744977, Fax: (01603) 744990

Location: village centre.
Credit cards: Mastercard, Visa, Switch, Amex.
Bitters: Flowers Original, Adnams, Marstons Pedigree, Boddington, Flowers IPA, 2 guests.
Lagers: Stella Artois, Heineken, Labatts.

Examples of bar/restaurant meals (lunch & evening, 7 days): *seafood crepe; home-made pies; roast honey & lime chicken; sausages & mash; lasagne; chilli; curry; steaks; fresh fish daily; mushroom & quorn casserole; veg. pie; duck-egg omelette; jacket potatoes; salads; sandwiches; many daily specials eg flaked crab crumble, large parrot fish in vine leaf & lemon grass with dill & ginger glaze, ragout of Norfolk hare, roast wild boar with sauce of port & woodland mushroom, ostrich, alligator, kangaroo! Chocolate delice; shortbread chantilly; bread & butter pudding. Children's menu. Trad. Sun. roasts.*

Much more than just a pub - The King's Head is a rarity, not just for the four squash courts and Crown Green bowls, but also for the highly creative and unusual food. Whether staunchly traditional, such as sausages and mash, or exotica like kangaroo or ostrich, all is fresh and prepared with pride by head chef Adrian and second chef Chris. The choice of beers and wines is also exceptional. The inn has stood by the river running through this quaint little village since 1602, and is full of character. No games machines assault the senses, neither do cigarettes in the no-smoking room. Lee Vasey plays live alternate Monday evenings, and there are numerous special themes and promotions. Landlady Pamela Wimmer is joined in the business by son Anton. Function room for up to 80. Children welcome. Sheltered courtyard.

NORFOLK — *What kind of rhino hangs over the bar?* — INNS & PUBS

THE UGLY BUG INN
Colton, nr Norwich. Tel: (01603) 880794

Location: in village
Credit cards: Mastercard, Visa, Switch, Delta, Eurocard.
Accommodation: 1 single (£27),
1 twin (en suite),
1 family with bathroom
(both £45). Tea & Coffee.
Bitters: Ugly Bug, Adnams, Old Speckled Hen, John Smith, 3 guests.
Lagers: Carlsberg, Kronenbourg.

Examples of bar/restaurant meals (lunch & evening, 7 days): *home-made paté; supreme of chicken stuffed with mozarella in wild mushroom sauce; salmon in puff pastry with lemon & parsley sauce; pie of the day; ravioli stuffed with ricotta & spinach; home-made black pudding pan-fried in garlic butter; lasagne; curries; steaks. Apple & marmalade crumble; lemon & mascarpone cheesecake; treacle pud; summer pud; quality Swiss ice creams. Trad. Sun. roasts £8.95.*

The odd name is not at all apt, for this striking conversion stands in over three acres of the most beautifully landscaped gardens (with barbecue), complete with carp stream and floodlit bridge. Inside, you will find it warm and congenial, replete with timbers, exposed brickwork and cottagey furniture. The restaurant seats 58 and there's also a conservatory for private parties, small wedding receptions etc. Since opening in 1991 Peter and Sheila Crowland have established a reputation for good, home-made food, including numerous ingenious and exotic dishes, plus an uncommonly good choice of wines and excellent ales, recognised by CAMRA and leading good beer guides. Children are welcome and the Dinosaur Park is nearby. Monthly quiz nights. Pitch and putt course planned for 1997!

THE HARE ARMS
Stow Bardolph, nr Downham Market. Tel: (01366) 382229, Fax: (01366) 385522

Location: off A10 between King's Lynn (9 miles) and Downham Market (2 miles).
Credit cards: Mastercard, Visa, Switch, Delta.
Bitters: Greene King.
Lagers: Kronenbourg, Harp.

Examples of bar meals (lunch & evening daily): *fresh fish daily eg rolled plaice fillet filled with spinach & tomato concasse in white wine cream sauce; home-made chilli; curry; lasagne; steaks; salads; sandwiches; daily specials eg skate wing in lemon butter sauce, pork steak in apricot sauce, spicy mixed bean bake with leek & cheese topping. Children's menu. Bar food served in restaurant Sunday lunchtimes.*

Examples of restaurant meals (a la carte Mon - Sat evenings, bookings advised): *paté profiteroles; lemon sole florentine; sea bass in paper parcel in white wine & julienne of vegetables; saffron chicken breast in spices with sauce of marinade & creme fraiche; beef smitan. Home-made fruit-filled meringue nests; hot pecan pie; chocolate torte. Also table d'hote (£16.75) Mon-Thurs evenings. Trad. Sun. roast.*

20 years under the same ownership, this popular ivy-clad inn in a pleasant little village has been recommended by Egon Ronay 15 years running for the delicious wholesome fare, and was also named Regional Pub of the Year 1993 in the Eastern Daily Press. Fresh local produce is used whenever possible - crab and lobster in summer, pheasant, pigeon and game in winter. The high-standard restaurant, a beautifully proportioned room, offers a menu of traditional and international dishes changed frequently. The 'Old Coach House' is available for a variety of functions, from private dinner or office parties to weddings (and family use on Sundays). Families are also welcome in the roomy conservatory or attractive garden. STOP PRESS: NATIONAL WINNER OF 'PUB CATERER OF THE YEAR' AWARD.

THE GREAT DANE'S HEAD
The Green, Beachamwell, nr Swaffham. Tel: (01366) 328443

Location: on village green, opp. church.
Credit cards: not acepted.
Bitters: Greene King Abbot, IPA, guest.
Lagers: Harp, Kronenbourg.

Examples of bar/restaurant meals (12 - 2:30pm, 7 -10pm, 7 days): *home-made steak & kidney pie; game pie; turkey & stilton pie; noisettes of lamb; steaks; traditional paella; Cajun chicken; chicken Wellington; spicy beef; seafood parcel; seafood tagliatelle; sweet & sour prawns; wing of skate; trout; game in season.*

The three pub signs will bewilder the unwary: one shows the head of a large dog; another that of a Viking; a third tells us this is 'The Hole in the Wall'. It was in fact once known as The Cooper's Arms, but as there was no bar beer was served through a hole in the wall. Well, this is Norfolk. And Beachamwell is one of the county's many secrets, for it's a lovely, unspoilt village in the middle of nowhere, distinguished by the only thatched church with a round tower in Norfolk - it's very, very old. The pub commands a perfect view of it over the classic village green. Built around 1820 (although the cellar is older), it has been refurbished by Frank and Jenny White, who have made it very popular for good, homecooked food in generous portions at reasonable prices. Staple favourites rub shoulders with the exotic, augmented by theme nights such as Thai. One can sit in the garden in summer. Pool table. B & B in village.

What was the cost of the Temperance Society excursion to Yarmouth in 1892?

THE CROWN HOTEL & RESTAURANT
Crown Road, Mundford. Tel: (01842) 878233

Location: village centre, just off A1065.
Credit cards: Mastercard, Visa, Diners, Amex.
Accommodation: from £29.50 sngl, £45 dbl; new Coach House with beautifully appointed rooms & Reception Room opened in Oct '95.
Bitters: Woodfordes Wherry & Nelson's Revenge, Websters, local-brewed Iceni beers, Sam Smiths, Directors.
Lagers: Fosters, Carlsberg, Holsten Export, Kronenbourg.

Examples of bar meals (lunch & evening, 7 days): *chicken breast with bacon & stilton cream; leek & gruyere strudel on fresh tomato sauce; home-made lamb kebabs; fresh fish (speciality) with classic & unexpected sauces; many daily specials eg Hungarian chicken, poached fillets of sea bream on bed of asparagus with light cream sauce, parcels of broccoli bound with pasta in smoked cheese & onion cream sauce. Deep apple bakewell; tiramisu; chocolate & almond torte.*

Examples of restaurant meals (as above): *scallop & mange tout salad; field mushrooms & hot garlic cottage prawns; noisettes of lamb with fresh mint & balsamic vinegar; sea bass fillet with smoked marlin. Trad. Sun. roasts. Booking always advised.*

NB: Open all day; food served 12 to 3pm, 7 to 10pm (last orders).

The Crown's recognition in the principal national guides is firmly based on the cooking - anything from home-made soups to a classic medley of Ickburgh duck, served in typical Norfolk portions, with prices starting at under £2. Many regulars have also been gained through 'Norfolk Pub Walks' (this being good walking country). In its time (from 1652) The Crown has also been a hunting lodge and doctor's surgery, and, perhaps uniquely in Norfolk, is built on the side of a small hill, so that one may walk in to the ground floor bar and exit from the first floor restaurant into the garden - glorious in summer. A lovely inn to stop off for good food, lively company and comfortable accommodation.

NORFOLK   *Which previous landlord dabbled in paints?*   INNS & PUBS

THE CROWN INN FREEHOUSE & RESTAURANT
Church Street, Gt Ellingham.Tel: (01953) 452367

Location: 80 yards past church.
Credit cards: Mastercard, Visa, Delta, Switch, Euro.
Bitters: Woodfordes, Adnams, Theakstons, John Smith, Websters, guest.
Lagers: Fosters, Miller, Kronenbourg.

Examples of bar/restaurant meals (lunch & evening, 7 days): unusual home-made pies; steaks; balti chicken; tagliatelle verdi with smoked bacon & cream; chilli; fresh fish direct from Lowestoft or Billingate; herb crepes filled with camembert cheese, seasonal veg. & tomato, basil & garlic sauce; salads (with h/m dressings & chutneys); omelettes; home-made baguettes; jacket potatoes; many daily specials eg grilled goats' cheese with Italian salami, duo of mallard & partridge casseroled with root vegetables & red wine. Home-made pancakes filled with fruit; choux pastry swan filled with chocolate mousse; jam roly poly; fruit pie. Children's menu. Trad. Sun. roasts.

Hats off to Justin Wilkins and chef Mark: despite a choice of 60-70 dishes, nothing on the main menu is bought in frozen and even the baguettes and chutneys are home-made. His three years here have helped make The Crown one of the most popular and respected eating houses in the area - a far cry from the days before the Wilkins family, who have lived in the village for generations, took over in 1989. Their remarkable success is prompting a new extension for spring '97, where diners will be able to enjoy a pre-dinner drink while scanning the huge menu. The patio will have a canopy and the beer garden landscaped. But the original building, 250 years old, timbered, with huge fireplace and resident spectral monk, will remain undisturbed. Regular wine-tasting events. Butterfly farm nearby.

THE BIRD IN HAND
Church Road, Wreningham. Tel: (01508) 489438

Location: village centre.
Credit cards: Mastercard, Visa, Amex.
Bitters: Adnams, Marstons Pedigree, Fullers London Pride, Boddingtons, weekly guest.
Lagers: Stella Artois, Heineken.

Examples of bar meals (12 to 2pm, from 6:30pm, 7pm Suns, until 10pm): *devilled sour cream prawns; Scottish smoked salmon; venison, pear & cranberry pie; aubergine-filled pasta with black olive dressing; stir-fried vegetables in creamy oyster sauce; roast skate wings with caper & gherkin butter sauce; haddock & 3-cheese pie; honey & minted roast rack of lamb; breaded Dublin Bay prawns.*

Examples from a la carte (12 to 2pm, 7 to 10pm, 7 days): *pan-fried red snapper with chilli sauce; French duck breast with blackberry & apple sauce; piri piri spiced fillet steak; haggis-stuffed guinea fowl supreme with whisky sauce; chestnut, asparagus, mange tout & baby corn pie; roast monkfish tails with garlic, bacon & mushrooms. Home-made desserts. Trad. Sun. roasts.*

This has emerged in recent years as one of the region's most talked about pubs, winning glowing praise from national publications and competition judges. Yet Carol Turner arrived seven years ago armed only with a training from the British Institute of Innkeeping and Norwich City College, and high expectations; now she has a staff of 30, including three chefs. The business continue to grow whilst maintaining the high standards of service and extensive menus on which its reputation has been built. The beautiful interior far surpasses the promise of the exterior, and is quite exceptional. The bar was once a stable, and that special farmhouse ambience is unmistakable; the restaurant is even called the Farmhouse, and is furnished most handsomely. Well behaved children welcome, and there's a large landscaped beer garden. Weddings and private parties a speciality. Conference facilites. Excellent washrooms.

NORFOLK *How many fishy stones are delivered fresh each week?* INNS & PUBS

THE OLD RAM
Tivetshall St Mary. Tel: (01379) 676794 Fax: (01379) 608399

Location: on A140 south of Norwich.
Credit cards: Mastercard, Visa, Switch.
Accommodation: 5 rooms (inc. 2 suites), all en-suite. Satellite TV, trouser press, hair dryer, direct phone, tea & coffee.
Bitters: Adnams, Woodfordes, Ruddles County, Boddingtons, Caffreys.
Lagers: Fosters, Holstein.

Breakfast served 7:30 to 11:30am daily. Examples of bar meals (11:30am - 10pm every day): *Ram grill; rack of pork ribs; barbecue chicken; trout with toasted almonds; steak & kidney pie; lasagne; mousakka; chicken curry; steaks; salads; filled rolls; filled jacket potatoes; aubergine & mushroom bake; legume mille feuille; extensive choice of chef's specials eg. pan-fried pork loin on stilton & port sauce, fillet of lamb on mint & mild mustard sauce; wide variety of fresh fish eg pan-fried monkfish tails on lime & ginger sauce, skate wings, whole baked turbot Large selection of desserts eg raspberry torte; fresh fruit cheesecake; chocolate ganache, chocolate fudge cake.*

No matter at what time, the car park of this 17th-century coaching inn seems always to be quite full - even at four in the afternoon! It is without doubt one of the most popular in the entire region, with a name that goes well beyond. The reasons are not hard to discern: as well as being open all day from 7:30am, the menu is enormous, and comprised of good, wholesome favourites, served in belt-loosening portions and in an amiable, lively atmosphere. Not surprisingly, then, it features in just about every major national guide, a credit to John Trafford, who with wife Julie has built this enviable success over the past nine years. Special occasions are honoured - roses for ladies on Valentine's Night, Beaujolais, Mothering Sunday, and others. Children welcome. Garden. No expense has been spared to make the accommodation quite superb.

THE WHITE HORSE INN
The Street, South Lopham. Tel: (01379) 687252

Location: on A1066 between Diss and Garboldisham.
Credit cards: Mastercard, Visa, Amex.
Bitters: Adnams, Greene King, guest.
Lagers: Carling, Harp, Kronenbourg.

Examples of bar meals (lunch & evening, 7 days): *steak & kidney pie; chicken, leek & stilton pie; chicken breast in honey & mustard sauce; pork tenderloin in cider & apple sauce; lamb in mint & redcurrant sauce; chicken tikka; plaice; cod; scampi; potato, cheese & onion pie; vegetable curry; hoagies; baguettes; salads; ploughman's; filled rolls. Granny's apple pie; toffee pecan pie; chocolate cheesecake; lemon meringue roulade. Trad. Sun. roasts.*

During their years at The Garden House, Bressingham, Gerald and Wendy Turner made it one of the best known and respected pubs in the region. Loyal followers were relieved to find they had moved just a mile or two down the road, and over the past two years they have begun to earn similar repute for The White Horse. As before, success has been built on good food at fair prices, but drinkers are always welcome. First, though, they had to renovate the 17th-century building (the staircase is actually Elizabethan), sensitive to the original timbers, exposed brickwork, inglenook fireplace and stripped wood floor. One may eat in either of the two bars, and children are welcome - they will prefer the garden with play equipment. Pool and darts inside. Very near the famous Bressingham Gardens and Steam Museum.

NORFOLK   *How many perches were on the Garboldisham Estate?*   INNS & PUBS

THE FOX INN
The Street, Garboldisham, nr Diss. Tel: (01953) 688151

Location: at crossroads of B1111 and A1066.
Credit cards: Mastercard, Visa, Amex, Switch, Delta, JCB.
   Bitters: Adnams Best, Broadside & Old Extra, Greene King IPA, guest.
   Lagers: Stella Artois, Heineken.

Examples of bar/restaurant meals (lunch & evening, 7 days): *local pheasant paté; black pudding fried with apple; crevettes grilled & basted with garlic & extra virgin olive oil; steak & mussel pie; chicken with Black Forest ham collar; hallormi kebabs in sun-dried tomato dressing; cider sausage; hoagies; cheesy tuna & pasta bake; potato skins; daily specials eg pan-fried smoked salmon with hollandaise, smoked gammon with honey glaze. Pavlova; lemon brulée; tiramisu.*

Glad tidings - The Fox is back! Once one of the region's best loved pubs, it sadly closed and fell into disrepair. Under new ownership since March 1996, it's now better than ever. None of the period character of the 1640 coaching inn has been lost: the timbers in snug, lounge and restaurant; the huge inglenook; terra cotta flooring; the nice view of the church; the ghost of a black labrador. One room has been designated no-smoking, and the conservatory is a family room, but one may eat anywhere - flexibility is a watchword, and petty rules are strictly forbidden! Barbecues are held ad hoc in the garden; darts and pool are indoor pastimes. Bressingham Garden and Steam Museum, Banham Zoo and Gt Ellingham Butterfly Farm are all within easy reach.

What is the licence number of the old tractor?

THE MILL INN
Bury Road, Market Weston, nr Diss. Tel: (01359) 221018

Location: on B1111 between Stanton and Garboldisham.
Credit cards: Access, Visa.
   Bitters: Old Chimneys (local), Adnams, Greene King.
   Lagers: Carlsberg, Kronenbourg.

Examples from lunch menu (Tues-Sun): *Sri Lankan beef curry; raised chicken & ham pie; smoked haddock & broccoli mornay; steak & stout pie; pasta provencale; salads from around the world; sandwiches; daily specials eg Dover sole Florentine, ham & leek roly poly with onion gravy; trad. Sun. roast plus 8 alternatives. Home-made fresh fruit pavlova; rum & raisin pie; chocolate brownie with chocolate custard; cherry brandy trifle; home-made ice creams.*

Examples from evening menu (Tues-Sat): *home-made venison paté; stir-fry prawns with mustard & coriander; duck breast with plum sauce; home-made vegetable ravioli & tomato sauce; steaks & grills: Turkish lamb; supreme of chicken stuffed with crab meat & coated with prawn & white wine sauce; daily specials.*

NB: closed ALL DAY Mondays except Bank Hols.

So many country pubs have either closed or fallen into the wrong hands of late that it is doubly refreshing to report one which gives cause to hope. Since taking over in September 1995, Mother and daughter Anne and Lesley Leacy (both with catering diplomas and experienced in the art) continue to make their mark with good, fresh, home-made food at very reasonable prices, served with a genuine friendliness in bar or dining room of their 18th-century former miller's home. The good-size menus are international enough, but monthly theme nights (usually on Thursdays) introduce diners to French, American, Curry etc specialities. For extra fun join in one of the car treasure hunts, or tour the 'Mill Trail' of local windmills. Children's dining room and garden. Outside catering service.

SUFFOLK *How many tons make 277160?* INNS & PUBS

THE WHITE HORSE
Old Newmarket Road, Risby. Tel: (01284) 810686

Location: near Bury St Edmunds on old A45, just off A14 (don't go into village).
Credit cards: Mastercard, Visa.
   Bitters: Bass, Worthington, Greene King IPA, Caffreys, guest.
   Lagers: Carling, Carling Premier, Grolsch.

Examples of bar meals (lunch & evening, 7 days): *king prawn kebabs; home-made soups; steaks with wide variety of sauces; steak & kidney pie; Thai stir-fry; Bradford chicken curry; sweet & sour pork; fajitas; scallops a la creme; rainbow trout a la Michel; veg. & nut stroganoff; baguettes; baked spuds; salads; daily specials eg grilled turbot. Majorcan ice creams (luxury); spotted dick; treacle pudding; fruit pudding. Trad. Sun. roasts.*

In a heartening reversal of current trends, this 300-year-old coaching inn is back in private hands after a spell under group management. Taking up the reins only in September 1996, Paul and Anne Wrightson have wrought a transformation with their genuine friendliness and stimulating menus. The pub itself won't have changed too much since judges called in to don their fine robes en route to Bury Assizes - large mirrors still adorn the walls, open log fires broadcast good cheer, and a timber lattice separates the dining lounge. Their worships would be less familiar with the rich carpet and plethora of RAF memorabilia. An August beerfest is planned, and red letter days such as Beaujolais Nouveau will be observed, but The White Horse Promise is that, given 48 hours notice, they will prepare any meal for your own special occasion! Children welcome - family room and sheltered garden with swings etc. Darts.

Who was the author of the wise maxim inscribed on a crossbeam?

THE TROWEL & HAMMER INN
Mill Road, Cotton, nr Stowmarket. Tel: (01449) 781234, Fax: (01449) 781765

Location: east side of village; from Stowmarket turn right off B1113 at signpost.
Credit cards: Mastercard, Visa, Eurocard, Delta, Switch, JCB.
Bitters: Adnams, Greene King, Nethergate, guest.
Lagers: Kronenbourg, Carlsberg.

Examples of bar meals (lunch & evening, 7 days): *filos of brie with creamy chive sauce; grilled sardines with herb butter; avocado salad with chicken & prawns; crab & herb pancakes; liver & bacon with onion gravy; fresh deep-fried cod with chips; steaks; kleftico; creamy leek, potato & stilton pie; steak, kidney & ale pie; ploughman's.*

Examples of restaurant meals (restaurant closed Sun. evenings & Mons): *terrine of salmon with watercress & dill; escalope of salmon with spinach & hollandaise sauce; confit of duck perigordin; fillet steak en croute. Pancakes with blackcurrants & cassis; chocolate & Cointreau mousse in brandy snap. Trad. Sun. roasts.*

This 15th-century freehouse, one of the best known and most picturesque in the region, was acquired in May '95 by Simon Piers-Hall (formerly of the wine trade) and Julie Huff (formerly of the celebrated Royal Oak, Yattendon). It is gratifying enough that it should continue as a family concern, but they have also introduced exciting menus, always freshly prepared despite their broad scope and daily revision, and accompanied by an outstanding wine list. In winter lovely open fires broadcast good cheer; in summer you may prefer to splash in the swimming pool in the large garden. There's also indoor pool - the kind played on a flat table. The cosy oak-beamed restaurant is well suited to private parties, and there's occasional live music. Well-behaved children welcome.

SUFFOLK *What was found in the car park during building works?* INNS & PUBS

THE BLACK HORSE INN
& STABLES RESTAURANT
The Street, Thorndon, nr Eye. Tel & Fax: (01379) 678523

    Location: 2 miles off A140 Norwich to Ipswich road at Stoke Ash.
    Credit cards: Mastercard, Visa, Delta.
        Bitters: Greene King Abbot & IPA, Woodfordes Wherry, Wexford, guest.
        Lagers: Kronenbourg, Carlsberg.

Examples of bar/restaurant meals (lunch & evening, 7 days): *steaks & grills; curry; chilli; lasagne; pasta shells with cheese & garlic sauce; steak & kidney pie; turkey paprika; scampi; plaice; mushroom stroganoff with cream & brandy; jacket potatoes; salads; sandwiches; many specials eg deep-fried brie, crispy coated vegetables with garlic & mayonnaise dip, wild boar casserole, pork & apple with cider & cream, venison casserole with port & cranberry (speciality), halibut steak with white wine & herb sauce. Vegan dishes by arrangement. Many home-made desserts. Children's menu. Trad. Sun. roasts.*

This 16th-century freehouse has one of the most extensive and innovative menus in the area. In addition to the time-honoured favourites, a long list of home-cooked specials is chalked on a blackboard. Vegetarians and even vegans are well looked after, fresh and crispy vegetables being a forte. The restaurant has been cleverly converted from stables, and the stalls are singularly conducive to intimacy and good conversation. In a friendly atmosphere (assisted by a log fire in winter), a warm welcome is extended to all (including families) by the staff. Children like to peer down the 42' well (covered by plate glass!) in the heavily timbered bar, and there's a lawned garden with seating. Occasional Morris Dancing and Pony and Trap meets. Beers notably fresh and well kept.

When did Annie and Arthur get married?

THE KING'S HEAD
High Street, Southwold. Tel: (01502) 724517

Location: main street, on right as approaching.
Credit cards: Mastercard, Visa.
Accommodation: 3 dbls/twins (non-smoking); all en-suite, TV, tea & coff;
from £50 per room; single rate by negotiation.
Bitters: Adnams.
Lagers: Stella Artois, Carlsberg.

Examples of bar meals (lunch & evening, 7 days): *local fresh fish simply grilled; steak, kidney & Guinness pie; Orford honeyroast ham; oak-smoked gammon; chicken & asparagus pie; curries; chilli; lasagne; charcoal grilled steaks, fish & chicken; pasta & vegetarian dishes always; jacket potatoes; ploughman's. Bakewell tart; fruit crumbles; sticky toffee pudding. Trad. Sun. roasts.*

Southwold is famed for its easy-going pace of life, and dining at this 18th-century town-centre pub is intended to be a casual, "come as you are" affair. Flexibility is the watchword: any reasonable request will be met, and as everything is prepared to order be ready to wait a little while in peak periods. Use the time to quaff some of the excellent Adnams ales or wines, which travel only a few yards from the brewery in the town (the pub has won the Adnams Cellar Award two years running), or study the pictures in the split-level timbered bar (formerly a grocery store). Sunday evenings are for Jazz and Blues buffs, when they are performed live. New bedrooms are very good value (as is the home-cooked food); take a brisk stroll to the beach before breakfast. Phil Goodacre is your genial host. Parking on street or nearby public car park.

THE CROWN AT WESTLETON
Westleton, Saxmundham. Tel: (01728) 648777, Fax: (01728) 648239
INTERNET E-MAIL: reception@the.crown.nemesis.co.uk

Location: village centre.
Credit cards: Access, Amex, Diners, Visa.
Accommodation: 17 doubles, 2 singles, private facilities & no-smoking in all. AA 2* 73%. Tourist Board 3 Crowns highly commended. Class 2 access for disabled.
Bitters: Adnams, Woodfordes Wherry, Black Sheep, 3 guests.
Lagers: Carlsberg, Red Stripe. Plus James White & Scrumpy Jack ciders.

Examples of bar meals (lunch & evening except Sat evenings): *very fresh fish of the day (min. 5 dishes, cooked in various ways - speciality); steak & kidney pie; pork casserole with cheese & herb dumplings; sirloin steak; vegetable & cashew nut bake; salads; sandwiches; daily specials. Raspberry & apple sponge pudding; sweet trolley.* Children's menu. Trad. Sun. roasts.

Examples from table d'hote menus (evenings only): *casserole of venison & apricots; kiln-roasted supreme of salmon with prawns & smoked mussels in champagne on delicate butter sauce; fruity vegetable & almond curry; daily specials eg poached fillet of brill in orange & ginger sauce.* Booking advised.

This picturesque village village has changed little, but Rosemary and Richard Price offer 'state of the art' amenities: six Honeymoon rooms, some with four-posters or half-tester beds, all equipped with superb bathrooms complete with jacuzzi. Barbecues are held weekend lunchtimes (weather permitting) in the pleasant terraced garden, and a large conservatory is for the use of non-smokers. Inside has an open log fire which spits and crackles on a cold day - just right for a bowl of soup and a hunk of granary bread, baked on the premises. World famous Minsmere Nature Reserve is just a few minutes' walk.

INNS & PUBS   *What is the mascot of the Victory Club?*   SUFFOLK

THE PLOUGH & SAIL
Snape Maltings, nr Aldeburgh. Tel: (01728) 688413

Location: on banks of River Alde.
Credit cards: Mastercard, Visa, Diners, Amex, Switch.
Accommodation: 2 self-catering cottages & 1 flat (weekly lets).
Bitters: Adnams, Kilkenny, guest.
Lagers: Carlsberg, Carlsberg Export.

Examples from menu (lunch & evening, 7 days): *Aldeburgh cod topped with cheddar; lamb provencal; pork fillet in cider & apple sauce; sausage pie; fish pie; steak & mushroom pie; ostrich; chicken tikka salad; mixed cheese fritters; deep-fried clams in tartare sauce; duck breast in cherry & liqueur sauce; mixed seafood pancakes; oriental dim sum with hoi sin sauce; ploughman's; sandwiches. Tropical summer pud; fruit & nut bombe; chocolate truffle cake; butterscotch fudge fruitcake; treacle & walnut tart. Sunday lunch carvery.*

One of East Anglia's top attractions, enjoying international celebrity as home of the annual Aldeburgh Festival (in June), the complex at Snape Maltings has everything to keep the family amused for at least a whole day: six different shops and galleries; river cruises; lovely walks; tea shop and restaurant; and this former maltsters' pub, family-run and recommended by leading national guides, well worth a visit on its own merit. Chalked daily on a board, the menus are as diverse as they are appetising, and may be enjoyed in characterful bar (with open log fire) or small dining room. Children are welcome; some might even like to play chess on the giant board in the garden. For further mind improvement, try the painting or craft courses. A wonderful location for a very 'different' week away from it all.

133

SUFFOLK

What type of food is froize?
(clue: it's not thin-cut chips)

INNS & PUBS

THE FROIZE INN
The Street, Chillesford, nr Woodbridge. Tel: (01394) 450282

Location: on B1084 Woodbridge to Orford road.
Credit cards: not accepted.
Accommodation: 3 dbls/twins, all en-suite, TV, tea & coff. £45 for 2 people.
Phone for details of midweek breaks.
Also caravan & camp site with full facilities - £6 incl. (tents £2).
Bitters: Own exclusive Nun-chaser, Nun-trembler, Nuns' Revenge; Adnams, Mauldons, Old Chimneys, Iceni, Woodfordes, weekly guests.
Lagers: Carlsberg, Kronenbourg.

Examples of bar/restaurant meals (lunch & evening Tues - Sun): *home-made fish pie; seafood pancake with crab sauce; Dover sole with tarragon & garlic; seafood ragout; hake in onion & garlic; steaks; fillet of halibut in wild mushroom sauce; deep-fried brie in plum coulis; vegetarian pancake; ploughman's; daily specials eg fresh scallops grilled with cheese & garlic butter, whole fresh grouse (in port, cranberry & brandy sauce).*
NB: closed all day Mondays (except Bank Hols)

Alistair and Joy Shaw made the King's Head at Orford one of the most popular and respected inns of the region. They left there in1994, but happily did not go far, buying this freehouse (just three miles away) in 1995. They have quickly caught the eye of national newspapers and guides again, particularly for the outstanding seafood and game. The inn has a fascinating history, being built on the site of a former friary at the head of Butley River. In times gone by the friars supplied weary travellers with a savoury froise (a sort of 15th-century take-away). Today a froize still features on the menu for modern walkers, cyclists, horsemen, birdwatchers (and motorists) who come to enjoy the Coastal Path, forestry and heathlands. Set in two acres of its own grounds, the inn has a large car park, camping and caravaning area, beer garden and children's play area. Great location for a stay, with lovely walks into and around Orford.

INNS & PUBS

*Which extremely rare bird is it possible
to see from the bar?*

SUFFOLK

THE RAMSHOLT ARMS
Dock Road, Ramsholt, nr Woodbridge. Tel: (01394) 411229

Location: off B1083 Woodbridge-Bawdsey road.
Credit cards: Mastercard, Visa.
Accommodation: 4 twins/dbls, £30pp B & B.
Bitters: Adnams, Flowers, Brakspears.
Lagers: Heineken, Stella Artois.

Examples of bar/restaurant meals (lunch & evening, 7 days, except Dec, Jan & Feb, when no food Sun evenings): *fresh oysters; warm salad of breast of woodcock & partridge with plum sauce; big bowl of fresh mussels with chips & mayonnaise; beef tomato with feta cheese, black olives & fresh basil. Fresh halibut pan-fried in olive oil; pot-roast partridge with red cabbage, bread sauce & game chips; platter of fresh local lobster, oysters, whole prawns & wild Irish salmon; Cromer crab; fillet of pork poached in cream with lime & juniper. Belgian chocolate mousse; sticky toffee pudding; fresh meringue; bread & butter pudding. Trad. Sun. roasts.*

Winner of the Egon Ronay "1997 Newcomer of the Year" award, this former shooting lodge and smugglers' inn is also bestowed with unparalleled views up and down the River Deben, being set by the beach at Ramsholt Dock. But paramount is the quality of the food; as much local produce as possible is used, and the daily-changing menu always includes fresh fish and game (in season). Children are welcome in the comfortable bar, which has a log fire, or the quieter dining room overlooking the river. Newly refurbished to a high standard, the bed-and-breakfast accommodation is going to be very sought after.

BUTT AND OYSTER
Pin Mill, Chelmondiston, nr Ipswich. Tel: (01473) 780764

Location: off B1456 Shotley Road.
Credit Cards: Mastercard, Visa, switch.
Bitters: Tolly Cobbold - on handpump or from barrel, from the reborn brewery across the river. Occasional guests.
Lagers: Stella Artois, Carlsberg.
Extended Hours: **Winter:** Mon-Fri 11am-3pm, 7pm-11pm; Sun 12 -3pm, 7pm-10:30pm.
Summer: Mon-Fri 11am-11pm. SUNDAYS 12-10:30pm in SUMMER; SATURDAYS 11am-11pm ALL YEAR.

Examples of bar meals (lunch & evening, 7 days): *lamb puffs; smoked haddock & prawn pot; smoked chicken, celery & walnut pie; spinach & ricotta cheese lasagne; fishermans pie; smoked chicken with onion & chive dip; savoury sausage pie; pork & apple pie; steak & kidney pie; tiger tail prawns; crispy curry pancakes; honey roast half duck; farm manager's lunch. Buffets at Saturday & Sunday lunch. Limited menus (rolls etc) outside main hours.*

Views of the River Orwell such as this are a major asset. However, not content to rest on nature's laurels, Dick and Brenda Mainwaring work at keeping the Butt and Oyster authentic. They succeed, as national guides and newspapers testify, and CAMRA named this the 'Regional Pub of the Year 1993.' The locals also treasure it, and the elders will confirm that it is unchanged over 60 years. Even the pub games, some almost forgotten elsewhere, live on here; juke boxes and the like do not. The view from the bar and dining room overlooks the boats and river, and at very high tides the river nearly overlooks them. There's an old smoke room with bare floorboards and smoke-stained ceiling. The home-made food varies daily and is of generous proportions. There's a children's room, or sit at tables by the river's edge.

THE COMPASSES INN
Ipswich Road, Holbrook. Tel: (01473) 328332, Fax: (01473) 327403

Location: on main road in village centre.
Credit cards: Mastercard, Visa, Diners, Amex.
Bitters: Benskins, Tetley, guest.
Lagers: Stella Artois, Carlsberg.

Examples of bar/restaurant meals (lunch & evening, 7 days): *crab bake; breaded mushrooms; paté; melon cocktail; kleftico; steaks; seafood & traditional lasagne; chilli bean bake; chicken curry; lemon chicken; home-made pies; fresh fish daily; smoked fishcakes; daily roast; cheese & vegetable slice in puff pastry; mushroom pancakes; jacket potatoes; salads; sandwiches; daily specials eg pork escalope Normandy, veal marengo, Italian quiche. Home-made puddings.*

Travellers once hired ponies here for the journey to Ipswich, which was a safer mode of transport than by boat on the River Orwell, to judge from the engraved ships' timbers dredged up and put on display. Also on display, hanging from the beams, are more than 1000 key fobs. Recent refurbishment has resulted in a more open-plan and spacious interior. Tables may be reserved in the light and airy dining area, but the stress is always on informality. However, what really makes the Compasses so popular are the generous portions of good food at very reasonable prices. Children are allowed and have a play area outside; grown-ups can relax in the garden or on the patio. In the same hands for over 16 years, the pub features regularly in national guides.

THE ANGEL INN

Stoke by Nayland, nr Colchester. Tel: (01206) 263245, Fax: (01206) 263373

Location: village centre.
Credit cards: Mastercard, Amex, Diners, Visa.
Accommodation: 6 doubles, all en-suite, TV, phone, hair dryer, tea & coffee; £59 per room incl. (£45 as sngl).
Bitters: Adnams, Greene King.
Lagers: Carlsberg, Kronenbourg.

Examples from lunch & supper menu (served daily in bar & Well Room, where table may be booked): *fresh dressed crab; home-made fishcakes; tomato & feta cheese salad; wild boar sausages; steak & kidney pudding; honey-glazed roast rack of lamb; saute of liver & bacon; griddled fresh wing of skate; steamed fillets of salmon & halibut; roast ballantine of duckling. Apple, apricot & sultana jalousse; raspberry & vanilla bavarois; syrup pudding. Trad. Sun. roasts. All is freshly prepared on the premises.*

'Which?' Suffolk Hotel of the Year 1997 is the latest in a long list of accolades (won over the past 11 years under current ownership), which include Egon Ronay's Pub Accommodation of the Year Award 1995 (for the whole country), and Suffolk Dining Pub of the Year in another major good food guide. The Angel is simply one of the most celebrated inns of the region, if not the entire country. Although the Georgian facade is attractive enough, it is but a prelude to the very splendid 17th-century interior. Looking for the most outstanding feature, one would settle on the gallery which leads from the tastefully appointed bedrooms to a view over the restaurant. A charming little lounge divides the bars from the two dining rooms, one of which has an ancient well. The village is a very pretty one, in the heart of Constable Country and just 15 minutes' drive from Colchester.

THE GEORGE & DRAGON
Hall Street, Long Melford. Tel: (01787) 371285, Fax: (01787) 312428

Location: centre of village, on main road.
Credit cards: Mastercard, Visa, Switch.
Accommodation: 2 sngls, 4 dbls/twins, 1 family; all en-suite, TV, direct phone. Special breaks by arrangement.
Bitters: Greene King, guest.
Lagers: Kronenbourg, Castlemaine.

Examples of bar/restaurant meals (lunch & evening, 7 days): *melon & prawn fan served on fruit sauce; game terrine. Swordfish steak on fresh lime sauce; halibut with white grapes in Muscadet sauce; roundels of lamb with hot mint sauce; pork & apple pie; kidney bordelaise; beef in Abbot ale; Suffolk sausages with onion gravy; smoked chicken with pasta; steaks; vegetarian dishes; sandwiches; daily specials. Desserts.*

NB: OPEN ALL DAY, EVERY DAY.

"Not a pub, not a restaurant, but a true village inn" - the words of Peter, Marilyn and Ian Thorogood, who've revived the art of innkeeping at their 16th-century coaching inn over the past 11 years. That means "no karaoke, discos, keg beer or men in over-sized suits drinking from bottles!" Instead, you have delicious and filling meals created in the kitchen from fine local produce, traditional local beers and superb French wines (clarets especially good). Entertainment, too, is traditional, with live music every Wednesday. Look out for special commemorative dinners - St George's Day, for example. Well behaved children are welcome, and there is a garden. An ideal base to stay; right in the heart of the region, Long Melford is England's longest village, a Mecca for antique collectors, and boasts two Tudor Halls and Suffolk's finest church. Recommended by most major pub guides.

SUFFOLK — *Who make up the duet at the piano?* — INNS & PUBS

THE ANGEL HOTEL
Market Place, Lavenham. Tel: (01787) 247388, Fax: (01787) 248344

Location: town centre.
Credit cards: Mastercard, Visa, Amex, Switch.
Accommodation: 7 dbls/twins, 1 family; all en suite, TV, phone, hair dryer, tea & coff;
from £60 per room (from £39.50 as sngl) incl. special winter breaks.
Bitters: Adnams, Nethergate, Mauldons, Greene King.
Lagers: Holsten, Carlsberg.

Examples of bar/restaurant meals (lunch & evening, 7 days): *warm salad of pigeon breast; smoked haddock bake; sausage cassoulet & granary bread; steak & ale pie; braised rabbit with white wine, tomatoes & rosemary; pheasant braised with cider & apples; grilled salmon fillet with pickled samphire; lamb in paprika & cream; sirloin steak; leek, tomato & lentil gratin. Raspberry creme brulée; Drambuie & oatmeal syllabub; chocolate roulade. Children's menu. Trad. Sun. roasts.*

Good Pub Guide's "Pub of the Year" and "Suffolk Dining Pub" (both 1997); Which? "Suffolk Hotel of the Year" 1995; an AA Rosette for cooking; regular inclusion in all the major national guides; more important, loyal customers who keep coming back - testimony to the high standards set over seven years by Roy and Anne Whitworth and John and Val Barry. Yet prices remain very reasonable indeed for such a location (on a corner of the famous market square, often used as a backdrop for historical movies), and the atmosphere always relaxed. Neither are children frowned upon; indeed, toys, high chairs, a no-smoking area and even friendly cats are all laid on! Older ones may appreciate the many board games provided, or even, one hopes, the classical pianist on Friday evenings. Look for the magnificent exposed Tudor fireplace and rare Tudor shuttered shop window. Barbecues in rear garden, tables and chairs to the front.

INNS & PUBS   *Why is this pub looked up to by the rest of Suffolk?*   SUFFOLK

THE PLOUGH
The Green, Rede, nr Bury St. Edmunds. Tel. (01284) 789208

Location: cul de sac, not far from church.
Credit cards: Mastercard, Visa.
Bitters: Greene King.
Lagers: Harp, Kronenbourg.

Examples of bar meals (lunchtime every day, & evenings except Sunday): *fresh fish (speciality); steaks; curries; salads; daily specials eg jugged hare in port & wine sauce; romany lamb with spaghetti & parmesan cheese; beef in horseradish sauce; chicken ham & stilton crumble.*

Examples of restaurant meals (evenings only, not Sundays. Traditional Sunday lunch): *pigeon breasts in Madeira & spinach; venison; trout; roast duck; veal in Dijon mustard & brandy; poached salmon; local game (speciality).*

Here in a quiet cul de sac by the village pub is the quintessential thatched country pub for which England is renowned, in the heart of some of Suffolk's finest countryside. Unlike some others, no disappointment awaits inside: the inglenook fireplace is an especially handsome one, the beams look good for another 500 years, and the fine collection of teapots strikes the right note without lapsing into tweeness. More importantly, the food is good and portions very substantial - The Plough has been a regular in good pub guides for years. Amiable hosts Brian and Joyce Desborough and staff foster an unstuffy, unhurried atmosphere, but in summer you may prefer the large sunny garden with a tropical aviary, a dovecote and ponies - children love it! They are welcome inside in the eating areas.

THE PLOUGH INN

Brockley Green, nr Hundon, nr Clare. Tel: (01440) 786789, Fax: (01440) 786710

Location:	1½ miles from Hundon towards Kedington (not to be confused with Brockley Green on the B1066); if in doubt, phone.
Credit cards:	Mastercard, Visa.
Accommodation:	7 twins/dbls, 1 family; all en-suite, teletext TV, phone, hair-dryer, trouser press, tea & coff; weekend breaks £175 for 2 people, 2 nights dinner, B & B. ETB 4-Crown; member of Logis; Caravan Club certified location.
Bitters:	local traditional ales, weekly guest.
Lagers:	rotating premier & standard.

Examples of bar meals (lunch & evening from 6pm, 7 days): *home-made soups; beef & Guinness pie; fresh fish; steaks; ploughmans.*

Examples of restaurant meals (as above): *lemon sole with prawns; duckling breast with orange; steaks; salmon poached in wine & cream; vegetarian dishes; seafood night every Tuesday. Trad. Sun. roasts (booking advised).*

Now in their 15th year here (it's been in the family over 30 years), David and Marion Rowlinson, ably assisted by Jim and Margaret Forbes, provide modern amenities (the restaurant is plush and air conditioned, for example) without sacrifice of old fashioned friendliness and charm. Soft red bricks and oak beams from an old barn engender a country pub atmosphere; this and good home cooked food (seafood a speciality) has won a place in local affections and a number of major guides. Not an easy one to find, but patience reaps its rewards. The views over the rolling countryside are alone worth the effort, and there is also a south-facing landscaped terrace garden. Well placed for Cambridge, Bury St Edmunds and Lavenham. Children welcome.

INNS & PUBS *Which famous batsman's great grandfather was a landlord here?* SUFFOLK

THE WHITE HORSE INN
Hollow Hill, Withersfield, nr Haverhill. Tel: (01440) 706081

Location: through village, turn by church, up the hill; or from the bypass turn at Withersfield signpost.
Credit cards: Mastercard, Visa.
Accommodation: (from late spring '97) 4 dbls/twins; all en-suite, TV, hair-dryer, tea & coff.
Bitters: Courage, John Smith, guest.
Lagers: Fosters, Kronenbourg.

Examples from lunch menu (Sat & Sun): *beef in Beamish pie; shepherds pie; macaroni cheese; bangers & mash; baguettes; salads; ploughman's; jacket potatoes; 3-course Sunday lunch with choice of roasts (speciality - booking advised). Home-made treacle sponge; apple & peach crumble; bread & butter pudding. Examples from evening menu (daily, booking advised): tiger prawns in garlic butter; home-made paté; petit poussin; rabbit pudding; steak & stilton; landlord's grill; fresh salmon; beef in Beamish pie.*

"Quality food, cooked simply" - the philosophy of Bernard and Cherry Lee, licencees since 1995, is straightforward but effective, and ever more visitors are beating a path to their picturebook 15th-century thatched cottage in one of Suffolk's handsomest villages, surprisingly overlooked despite providing a backdrop to TV's Lovejoy series. Inside is cosy and cottagey, full of engaging oddities such as the ancient horngram in the dining room. From here French doors lead out to a pleasant garden. To the other side, an old cart lodge has been converted to quality accommodation, in an area which badly needs it. Bernard worked many years in the brewing industry, but is especially proud to present an exceptional and good-value wine list. Marquee for functions.

THE THREE BLACKBIRDS
Ditton Green, Woodditton, nr Newmarket. Tel: (01638) 730811

Location: village centre.
Credit cards: Mastercard, Visa, Delta, Switch.
Bitters: Greene King, Kilkenny, guest.
Lagers: Carlsberg, Stella Artois.

Examples of bar/restaurant meals (lunch & evening except Sun. evening): *filo pastry filled with smoked salmon mousse on bed of gravlax; lamb provencal terrine; mille-feuille of steamed courgettes; half barbary duckling in cherry sauce; braised steak in Suffolk ale suet pud; oven-roasted chicken livers on black pudding with apple & herb sauce; warm tartlet of wild mushrooms & avocado; daily specials eg chicken & mushroom basket, trio of fresh fish. Warm chocolate & walnut tart; home-made summer fruits meringue; plus supporting menu. Trad. Sun. roasts.*

Don't expect the ordinary; as the examples listed above indicate, the cooking here would do credit to a top West End restaurant - chips are taboo! But being 'up-market' does not mean being stiff and stuffy; the atmosphere remains warm, friendly and relaxed, as befits a 17th-century village pub. Serious epicures should join the Blackbird Diners' Club - monthly theme nights which might include wine or whisky tasting with a menu to match - introduced by the new owners (since April '96). Naturally the horse racing theme is celebrated in the decor, but there also old photos and poems reflecting village life. Restaurant available for hire. Petanque in garden. Families welcome.

THE OLIVER TWIST
High Road, Guyhirn, nr Wisbech. Tel: (01945) 450523

Location: on A47, near Guyhirn Bridge.
Credit cards: Mastercard, Visa, Amex.
Bitters: Everards Beacon & Tiger, guest.
Lagers: Carling, Budweiser.

Examples of bar meals (lunch & evening, 7 days): *steaks & grills; steak & mushroom pie; rogan josh; tandoori chicken; Chinese barbecue ribs; sweet & sour chicken balls; duckling a l'orange; salmon & prawn mornay; battered plaice/cod; mussels in garlic.*

Examples of restaurant meals (every evening, plus trad. Sun. lunch): *scampi provencale; steak Diane; chicken chasseur; mixed grill; aromatic lamb; lemon sole in prawn sauce; poached salmon with lobster sauce; macaroni passana. Banoffi pie; chocolate snowballs; fresh fruit salads/flans.*

NB: The arrival of two experienced new chefs in Feb. '97 will mean substantially revised menus.

'British Champion Cellarman of the Year (1995)' is the latest in a series of such awards to go to new licensees (since Oct. '96) Mick and Jacqui Thornton, achieved over six years at The Railway, Ratby (Leics). Mick has been in the trade over 30 years and takes great pains to serve beer in the best possible condition. Jacqui has a professional cooking qualification, and they've recently been joined by son John, also a chef - Ratby's loss is Fenland's gain! As well as innovative menus, they organise monthly banquets, such as Chinese or Medieval. The pub is much older than first appears, and was a coaching inn on the banks of the River Nene (good fishing). Inside is warm and hospitable, and the open brick fireplaces and timbered walls and ceilings confirm its antiquity. The dining room can accommodate functions (like wedding receptions) for up to 50. Since the by-pass the location is much quieter and parking easier. Lovely Peckover Hall nearby.

NEW SUN INN & RESTAURANT
20 High Street, Kimbolton. Tel. (01480) 860052

Location: on main street, village centre.
Credit cards: Mastercard, Visa, Switch, Delta.
Bitters: Charles Wells, Old Speckled Hen.
Lagers: Red Stripe, McEwans.

Examples of bar meals (lunch & evening, except Sun. & Mon. evenings): *steak & kidney pudding (speciality); pork & leek sausage; home-made picnic pie; chicken, asparagus & wine pie; chicken & mushroom lasagne; chilli; fresh fish dishes; mushroom stroganoff; jacket potatoes; doorstep sandwiches. Jam roly poly; bread, butter & brandy pudding; spotted dick; banana brulé; Belgian chocolate ice cream.*

Examples of restaurant meals (as above): *lobster thermidor; steaks; pork stroganoff; chicken stuffed with smoked salmon in white wine sauce; magret of duck; rack of lamb; vegetarian pasta of the day; daily specials eg Grafham fresh trout in pink peppercorn sauce; grouse sauted in wine. Hot chocolate fudge & walnut pudding (speciality). Trad. Sun. roasts.*

NB: OPEN ALL DAY SUNDAY

Kimbolton is one of the region's most striking and historic villages, dominated at one end by Kimbolton Castle, once home to Catherine of Aragon (she died there) but now a school (open to the public at certain weekends). King John initiated the 'Statute Fair' (known as 'Statty Fair') in the 13th century; it's still held in the main street on the third Wednesday of September, on condition that if it misses a year it can never be held again. But neither should one miss a visit to this unusual 16th-century hostelry, recently acquired by Steve and Elaine Rogers. Despite the breadth of the menu, food is home-made, served in the modern conservatory or ancient restaurant. Look out for 'ram-roasts' on the patio, or theme nights, such as Italian. Children welcome. Easy parking on street.

INNS & PUBS   *What is the connection with a famous steam engine?* CAMBRIDGESHIRE

THE EATON OAK
Crosshall Road, Eaton Ford, St Neots. Tel: (01480) 219555, Fax: (01480) 407520

```
     Location: at junction of A1 with B645.
  Credit cards: Mastercard, Visa, Eurocard, Amex.
 Accommodation: 9 dbls/twins; all en-suite, phone, satellite TV, tea & coff.
       Bitters: Charles Wells Eagle, Fargo & Bombardier.
        Lagers: Red Stripe, McEwans.
```

Examples of bar meals (lunch & evening, 7 days): *chicken breast with stilton & bacon wrapped in puff pastry; steak au poivre; minted lamb steak; curry; chilli; lasagne; steak & kidney pie; Covent Garden pie; veg. tikka masala; oak-smoked haddock poached in milk & butter; ploughman's; sandwiches.*

Examples of restaurant meals (as above): *crispy coated brie in orange sauce; Japanese prawns; smoked seafood platter; steaks & grills; Cajun chicken; fresh fish; salmon en croute. Pear William shortcake; summer fruit pudding; apple strudel; raspberry meringue surprise. Trad. Sun. roasts.*

NB: Food available ALL DAY SUNDAY.

Charles Wells Brewery prefers its managed houses to be individual rather than formulaic; being family-run, this one is no exception. Value and quality are the watchwords; food is freshly prepared and chalked daily on a blackboard. This former 18th-century farmhouse has been refurbished in style: thick carpeting and upholstery, wood panelling, brick arches, quality prints. The conservatory restaurant (available for functions) is especially attractive, with its small elevated 'galleries'. The normal laid-back atmosphere gives way now and again to live jazz, quiz nights and special occasions such as New Year and Beaujolais Evening. Well appointed accommodation is in a separate block, is well placed for local attractions like Grafham Water, and is only one hour from London. Children welcome. Small patio to front.

CAMBRIDGESHIRE — *Which colourful gardener used to sup here?* — INNS & PUBS

KING WILLIAM IV
High Street, Fenstanton, nr St Ives. Tel: (01480) 462467

Location: village centre, by clock tower.
Credit cards: Mastercard, Visa, Amex, Delta, Switch.
Bitters: Greene King.
Lagers: Harp, Kronenbourg, Stella Artois.

Examples from lunch menu (7 days): *home-made lasagne; steak & kidney pudding; beef stroganoff; steaks; venison steak with mushroom, cream & brandy sauce; liver & onions; lemon chicken; salads; jacket potatoes; daily specials eg fresh grey mullets barbecued with garlic & olive oil, huntsman's grill, stuffed peppers. Trad. Sun. roasts. Spotted dick; treacle & walnut pud; Baileys cheesecake; sticky toffee pudding; summer pudding.*

Examples from evening menu (not Sunday evenings): *salmon timbales; escargots; breast of duck with hot apricot sauce; turkey crepes; rack of lamb with parsley & mustard crust; pork medallions sauteed with apple & cider sauce; many dishes as above.*

NB: open ALL DAY Sundays.

Not only did a celebrated landscape gardener (see 'trivia' above) use this as his local; Oliver Cromwell was once the local squire. Were they to meet for a pint today they would be surprised to find how little has changed: antique furniture, original beams and lattices, three brick inglenooks, low ceilings. But it is the kitchen, where three chefs toil to produce a wide choice of fresh home-cooked food, which has won a regular place in the main national guides. The landlord is now in his 10th year here, which also speaks volumes. Wednesday is live Jazz and Blues Night - there is a no-smoking room. Petanque planned for garden.

Which Rosebud raised Cain in 1876?

THE TRINITY FOOT
Huntingdon Road, Swavesey. Tel: (01954) 230315

Location: A14 (formerly A604) Eastbound, 7 miles west of Cambridge.
Credit cards: Visa, Mastercard.
Bitters: Flowers, Boddingtons, Whitbreads.
Lagers: Stella Artois, Heineken.

Examples of bar meals (lunchtime 7 days, every evening except Sunday): *fresh fish at most times; fresh lobster from tank; samphire in season; queen scallops mornay; oysters au gratin; tiger prawns in garlic butter; John Dory; guinea fowl in red wine sauce; grilled mackerel Portuguese style; monkfish with Pernod & cream; steaks; mixed grill; curry; omelettes; salads. Sherry trifle; meringues glace; banana split; peach melba. Seasonal daily specials eg samphire, lobster, crab.*

Seafood is much in evidence - the pub has its own adjacent fish shop, supplied from Lowestoft, Humberside and Loch Fyne. Also unusual, unique in fact, is the name Trinity Foot, after a pack of beagle hounds mastered by Colonel Whitbread, whose family's beer is on sale here. The hunters eschewed the usual fox as quarry, preferring hares, sportingly pursued on foot. 'Trinity' of course refers to the nearby university college. John and Brenda Mole will serve you delicious freshly prepared food in portions to satisfy the most ardent trencherman, with special evenings like French, Spanish or Portuguese to add a little zest. Well-behaved children are welcome in the eating area or unleashed onto the large, safe lawn, and there's also a conservatory. Despite its proximity to the A14, traffic is high up on an embankment and is not too intrusive. Large car park. Featured in national good pub guides.

CAMBRIDGESHIRE   *To what name does the parrot answer?*   INNS & PUBS

THE RED LION FREEHOUSE
High Street, Hinxton, nr Cambridge. Tel: (01799) 530601, Fax: (01799) 531201

Location: vilage centre.
Credit cards: Mastercard, Visa.
Bitters: Adnams, Bass, Boddingtons, Greene King IPA.
Lagers: Carling, Grolsch.

Examples of bar/restaurant meals (lunch & evening, 7 days): *deep-fried mini camembert in gooseberry sauce; stilton & white port paté; skate wing in butter & lemon juice; two halibut steaks with parsley butter; Whitby Bay scampi; roast duck bigarade with orange & Grand Marnier sauce; beef stroganoff; chicken Kiev; rainbow trout stuffed with prawns; steaks; Thai 10-veg. curry; many daily specials eg chicken dupiaza, lamb & apricot pie, Mexican chilli pork, spicy deep-fried prawns, leek & mushroom pasta bake. Banoffee meringue roulade; jam roly poly; apricot bread & butter pudding; dark chocolate & Cointreau royale. Trad. Sun. roasts plus alternatives.*

Just a short detour off the M11 will take you to this very pleasant village with its handsome 16th-century coaching inn. Rated highly by a leading national good pub guide, food is home-cooked by a talented chef (vegetarians will be well pleased), and all is spotlessly clean and most inviting - why do people use plastic roadside eateries? It's also near enough to Cambridge to combine with a day's shopping or sightseeing, and would break up a journey from Norfolk to London very nicely. The tasteful restaurant extension is light and airy with vaulted ceiling, and there's also a small drinking bar. Staff include an Amazonian parrot who likes to engage visitors in conversation, and a pony in the garden. Their bosses are Jim and Lynda Crawford, now in their 13th year.

THE PLOUGH
High Street, Gt Chesterford. Tel & Fax: (01799) 530283

Location: 1 mile from M11/A11 junction, near Saffron Walden.
Credit cards: Mastercard, Visa, Delta, Switch.
Bitters: Greene King Abbot & IPA, Wexford.
Lagers: Kronenbourg, Stella Artois, Harp.

Examples from lunch menu (daily): *baguettes; huffers; hoagies; jacket potatoes; sandwiches; ploughman's; steak in French bread; pie of the day; ham & eggs; daily specials eg chicken tikka masala, giant Yorkshire puds filled with sausages or beef, hot roast beef sandwiches, fisherman's pie. Trad. Sun. roasts.*

Examples from evening menu (Thurs - Sat): *mushrooms stuffed with stilton; home-made paté; roast rack of lamb with garlic & rosemary sauce; steak with mushrooms & red wine sauce; plaice with prawns & white wine sauce; battered cod & chips; tuna pasta bake; daily specials. Home-made cheesecake; apple pie; gateaux.*

The licencee is new (since Oct. '96), but the timeless traditions of honest pub food, fine ales and warm hospitality continue. It's also a strikingly handsome building, perhaps more so inside than out, recent renovation having done nothing to destroy its 17th-century period character. Of special note are the two magnificent inglenooks in bar and restaurant. Fittingly, old farming implements adorn the ancient timbers. Indoor pastimes, apart from good conversation, are pool, darts and shoveha'penny - the Games Room doubles for functions. Children are welcome and have a playground and grassed area in the 160 yd garden. Audley End House is very near; Anglesey Abbey and Wimpole Hall are a short drive.

THE AXE AND COMPASSES.
Arkesden, nr Saffron Walden. Tel: (01799) 550272

Location: village centre.
Credit cards: Mastercard, Visa.
Bitters: Greene King IPA & Abbot.
Lagers: Kronenbourg, Harp.

Examples of bar meals (lunch & evening, 7 days): *homemade steak & kidney pie; sirloin steak; pork loin on a mushroom & cream sauce topped with stilton; moussaka & garlic bread; moules mariniere; skate; king prawns; cod; plaice; sandwiches; ploughman's.*

Examples of restaurant meals (as above): *roast duck breast; wild venison in brandy redcurrant sauce; chicken, leek & bacon crumble; seafood & game in season; tenderloin of pork with mushroom sauce & stilton; fresh fish dishes; wild mushroom pancake; stir-fry vegetables with mustard sauce in pastry case. Trad. Sun. roasts £10.50 (4 courses).*

NB Children eat at half price.

Newcomers to Arkesden wonder why they've never heard of it before. It is, quite simply, exquisite, and puts many a more famous place to shame. Grand old thatched houses straddle a little stream in the dappled shade of willow trees. For complete perfection a lovely old country pub is required, and 'The Axe and Compasses' fulfills the role admirably - a picturebook 17th-century house, presided over by owner Themis Christou and family. They foster a notably relaxed and unhurried atmosphere, aided by crackling fires in winter, so linger a while and savour the home cooking. Seafood lovers should note that Tuesday is FISH NIGHT. Star rating in national good pub guide. Children welcome in restaurant and patio areas. Definitely not one to be missed!

What was the burning issue here at the turn of the century?

THE CROWN
Elsenham, nr Bishop's Stortford. Tel: (01279) 812827

Location: village centre.
Credit cards: Mastercard, Visa, Diners, Amex, JCB.
Bitters: Crouch Vale Millennium Gold, Tetleys, guest (changed regularly).
Lagers: Carlsberg Export, Castlemaine, Carlsberg.

Examples of bar meals (lunch & evening daily except Sundays): *deep-fried bread baskets with various fillings; savoury stuffed pancakes; seafood mixed grill; sautéd chicken livers in crepe basket; steak & kidney pie; lamb turino; duck Marco Polo; fisherman's pie; vegetable lasagne; pork T-bone in Calvados; local fresh trout in shellfish sauce; steaks; daily specials eg barbecue ribs, fresh plaice filled with crab & prawns, casseroles. Lunch only: homemade Crown burgers; Braughing sausages (noted); chicken tikka; hot rib of beef. 15 home-made ice creams.*
Menu revised regularly.

The sheer extent and originality of the menu makes it all the more amazing that everything, even the ice cream, is home-made and fresh. This has not escaped the notice of most of the main national guides and especially that of local people, so booking is advised at peak times. All is of course cooked to order, but there are a number of quick items listed for those in a hurry at lunchtime. Around 350 years old, formerly three cottages and then a coaching inn (royalty is said to have stayed here), its antiquity can be seen in the split-level bar, with its old timbers and open fire, next to which is the intriguing 'Dingly Dell', a floral fantasy. Activity comes in the form of monthly quiz nights, darts and dominoes. Well behaved children welcome - swings in garden. Dining room available for wedding receptions (and funerals!). The patience and good humour of licensees Ian and Barbara Good is witnessed by over 20 years of pulling pints here.

ESSEX — *Who is on the waggon (apart from the landlord)?* — INNS & PUBS

THE WAGGON & HORSES
High Street, Gt Yeldham, nr Halstead. Tel & Fax: (01787) 237936

Location: on A604, 200 yds from famous Yeldham Oak.
Credit cards: Mastercard, Visa, Delta, Switch, Amex, Diners.
Accommodation: 1 sngl, 5 dbls/twins. TV, tea & coff. c/h. £15pp incl Cont. brkfst. Rooms are 16th-century.
Bitters: Greene King, 1 regional & 1 national guest.
Lagers: Harp, Kronenbourg.

Examples of bar snacks (lunch & evening, 7 days): *deep-fried potato skins; scampi; plaice (with hand-cut chips); doorstep sandwiches; ploughman's.*

Examples of restaurant meals (as above): *home-made soup; avocado with bacon & tomato salad; steak & kidney pudding; lambs' liver & black back bacon; strips of barbary duck with ginger & honey; chicken breast with creamy mushroom sauce on buttered taglatelle; 'Joe Blake' sirloin steak. Trad. Sun. roasts £9.95 (3 courses).*

The eye-catching painted waggon to the front was the Rolls Royce of its day; built in 1840, it is one of the oldest in the country. Another outmoded transport is the nearby Colne Valley Steam Railway. Being 'Lovejoy Country' the area has an association with antiques, with many fine buildings, of which this former three 16th-century cottages is one. Two ghosts are said to walk the timbered, split level bar, one of them a lady who apparently objects to war memorabilia but not the many Punch cartoons with amusing modern 'punch lines'. Young chef Ellie Cox is highly regarded in the area, and her cooking utilises as much fresh and local produce as possible. Young and affable landlord Mike Shiffner has built a thriving business since Nov. 1994, and plans further improvements. Games Room has pool, darts and shove ha'penny; garden has boules. Children welcome. Accommodation is remarkably good value.

Where will you find a duck here?

THE KING'S HEAD
The Street, Gosfield, nr Halstead. Tel: (01787) 474016

Location: main road, village centre.
Credit cards: Mastercard, Visa, Diners, Delta, Switch.
Bitters: Boston Beer, Marstons Pedigree, Poachers, Flowers IPA, Boddingtons.
Lagers: Stella Artois, Heineken.

Examples of bar/restaurant meals (lunch every day, evenings Tues - Sat): *home-made steak & kidney pudding; liver & bacon; stew with dumplings; game pie; chicken & mushroom pie; T-bone steak; red snapper; fresh salmon; monkfish thermidor; shark steak; chicken in prawn & Pernod sauce; steak in stilton sauce; lamb in apricot sauce; pheasant in berry & port sauce; old favourites. Trad. Sun. roasts.*

The 40-seater candlelit conservatory restaurant (with festoon blinds) is a fine setting for a memorable meal, and new licensees Lee and Julie Hughes firmly intend to make it one of the best known and respected in the area. They and their staff generate a happy, easy-going atmosphere, notwithstanding the spirit of a man who hanged himself here - incredibly, this 15th-century timber-framed building was once a police station, and the door to the cells is still there in the bar. A musician plays live in conjuction with Friday Feast Nights, which could be for example Curry, Chinese, Italian, Mexican - eat as much as you can for £7.50. There are also ad hoc theme evenings - GI Night and Caribbean are recent examples. Children are welcome, and a playground and ballpark are under construction, ready for 1997. Hedingham Castle and Gosfield Lakes (with water skiing) are very close.

ESSEX   *Where is the rent going?*   INNS & PUBS

THE GREEN MAN
Gosfield, nr Halstead. Tel: (01787) 472746

Location: on Braintree to Hedingham road.
Credit Cards: Mastercard, Visa, Amex, Diners, Switch, Delta.
Bitters: Greene King.
Lagers: Kronenbourg, Castlemaine.

Examples of bar meals (lunchtime 7 days, every evening except Sunday): **Evenings:** *game soup with sherry; breaded mushrooms with garlic butter; Dover sole; oxtail ragout; steaks; boiled beef & carrots; roast duck with orange sauce; plaice fillets with prawn sauce; steak & kidney pudding; selection of home-made fresh vegetarian dishes (eg spinach pancakes, vegetable lasagne).* **Lunchtime:** *Cold buffet; hot dish of the day. Choice of home-made desserts.*

'Essex Dining Pub of the Year 1995' is a recent accolade from a leading national good pub guide for the best traditional food in the county. Nothing is frozen; all is cooked to order - special requests catered for if possible. You may not be able to resist the succulent array of cooked meats, shellfish, salmon and more on the buffet table, and speciality evenings - eg Italian, Greek, Curry, Fish - are also very popular, so booking is advised. It's refreshing to see staff so well turned-out, courteous and hard-working. Tellingly, most have worked for proprietor John Arnold for many years, including his 'right-hand lady', Janet Harrington, now in her 26th year here. It is these 'old-fashioned' virtues which endow this 16th-century pub with uncommon warmth and civility. Children are tolerated if well behaved; if not there's a rather nice garden by the large car park. Small room for private functions.

INNS & PUBS   *Who once drank from the plant-holder*   ESSEX
              by the restaurant entrance?

THE GREEN DRAGON

Upper London Road, Young's End, nr Braintree. Tel: (01245) 361030, Fax: (01245) 362575

Location: A131 2 miles south of Braintree - nr Essex showground.
Credit cards: Visa, Mastercard, Diners, Amex.
Bitters: Greene King Abbot & IPA. Bottled selection.
Lagers: Harp, Kronenbourg.

Examples of bar meals (lunch & evening, 7 days): *home-made pies; Suffolk hotpot; steaks; veal in mustard sauce; smoked salmon & prawn risotto; fresh fish & shellfish daily; trad. roasts; Indian-style chicken; fillet of salmon en croute; leek, mushroom & potato cakes; chicken & bacon parcels; vegetarian specials; daily blackboard specials.*
Examples of restaurant meals (as above): *sea bass roasted with prawn & leek sauce; skate wings pan-fried with capers; Bradon rost (hot smoked fillet salmon with whisky sauce); turkey Alexander; roast duckling with Cointreau sauce; chicken Wellington; beefsteak, kidney & mushroom pie; kleftiko; steaks; brown rice & hazelnut loaf. Trad. Sun. roasts.*

Bob and Mandy Greybrook have been at the Green Dragon for over 11 years, during which time it has become one of the most popular pubs in the area (the large car park is a necessity) and the recipient of numerous catering awards. Fresh seafood - langoustines and salmon from Scotland, oysters and wetfish from nearby Mersea - has increasingly become a speciality. The 48-seater restaurant was converted from a barn, serving a la carte and fixed-price menus, plus a Sunday roast menu throughout the day - bookings always advised. Or just drop by for a meal in the cosy bar or snug. The garden has a play area with aviary. Private parties and weddings catered for.

ESSEX — *By what name was the pub formerly known?* — INNS & PUBS

THE Du CANE ARMS
The Village, Gt Braxted, nr Witham. Tel: (01621) 891697

Location: village centre.
Credit cards: Mastercard, Visa, Delta, Switch.
Bitters: Greene King IPA, Adnams, Websters, John Smith, guest.
Lagers: Carlsberg, Fosters, Holsten.

Examples of bar meals (lunch & evening, 7 days): *fresh fish of the day (chef's own beer batter); home-made steak, kidney & mushroom pie; beef midani; chicken princess; lasagne; steaks; trout; caprisciosa fettucini (seafood); salads; sandwiches. Home-made fruit crumbles; treacle pud; spotted dick; chocolate pud; gateaux.*

Examples of restaurant meals (as above): *smoked eel smetana; mushroom bourgignon; beef stroganoff; ragout of scallops & crayfish; salmon parcel; breast of duckling oriental style; steak midani; vegetable midani (midanis a speciality). Trad. Sun. roasts.*

NB: Bar meals may be enjoyed in restaurant on weekdays for a £1 cover charge.

Fresh herbs from the garden, fresh-baked rolls from the oven, interesting and predominantly home-made food (the uncommon midani dishes are particularly popular): The Du Cane Arms is drawing custom from a wide radius to this out-of-the-way village. The Hyde family - Eric and Brenda, Alan and Angela - came here in spring 1991 with many years of experience. Their high standards refreshingly extend to a ban on foul language. There has been an inn on the site since 16th century, when the Du Canes were the local gentry, but this one dates from the 1930s, and is light and airy, with pot plants in the L-shaped bar, fresh flowers in the restaurant (which also serves for functions up to 30). Children welcome. Small garden. Pottery opposite, Braxted Hall and golf course nearby.

What is the weight of the pike?

THE GREEN MAN
Howe Street, nr Chelmsford Tel: (01245) 360203

Photo courtesy Priory Photographic of Chelmsford

Location: on main road, north side of village.
Credit cards: Mastercard, Visa, Switch, Eurocard, Delta.
Bitters: Ridleys, John Smith's.
Lagers: Carlsberg, Fosters, Holsten Export.

Examples of bar meals (lunch & evening, 7 days): *garlic mushroom hotpot; smoked haddock with poached egg; fresh battered cod; home-cooked ham; h/m steak & kidney pie; liver, bacon & onions; steaks; lamb chops with mint sauce; jacket potatoes; ploughman's; sandwiches; daily specials eg chicken in stilton & broccoli sauce, half roast duck in orange sauce, sausage & beef hotpot, fresh whole plaice. H/m apple pie; treacle tart; mandarin cheesecake; chocolate roulade; lemon brulée. Children's menu. Trad. Sun. roasts.*

"The oldest pub in Essex" - parts of it date from the 14th century - stands in five acres by the River Chelmer, with fishing rights, and in good walking and cycling country - route maps available for small donation to local hospice. But it is another outdoor pursuit, horseracing, which is evidently an interest of ex-farmer Richard Bailey, a local man who 'took up the reins' as landlord on July 4th, 1995. His brother Kim is a professional trainer, and you could join a syndicate to buy and maintain a horse. Other innovations are in the pipeline, including facilities for business breakfasts and lunches, live jazz (with special menus) on Monday nights, and a room equipped with games for children. They will also approve of the play area and aviary in the garden. One young lad apparently likes it here so much that his spirit is reluctant to leave! Once ensconsed in the warm, cosy, timbered dining room or lounge, warmed by an open log fire, and after a good 'farmhouse-size' home-made meal, you may feel the same. Weddings and private functions welcome.

Name the games on the chimney breast.

THE BLACK BULL FREEHOUSE
Dunmow Road, Fyfield, nr Ongar. Tel: (01277) 899225

Location: on B184 Ongar to Dunmow road.
Credit cards: Mastercard, Visa, Switch.
Bitters: Wadworth 6X, Courage Directors, Ruddles, John Smith.
Lagers: Fosters, Carlsberg, Kronenbourg.

Examples of bar/restaurant meals (lunch & evening, 7 days): *soft roes on toast; guacamole; homemade barbecued ribs; tenderloin of pork with chillies; skate with lèmon butter; steak & kidney pudding; steaks; daily specials. Fish night on Thursdays. Lunchtime only: jacket potatoes; variety of ploughmans; sandwiches; specials.*

The Black Bull is widely regarded as being one of the best pubs for food in these parts, so booking ahead is always advised at busy times. Proprietor (for 20 years!) Alan Smith has achieved this status by taking great pains to preserve high standards - deep frying is frowned on, and the menus are highly original, even exotic, and prepared with skill. The emphasis is on fresh meats, fish and vegetables, 'gently' influenced by chillies, garlic, coriander and other spices! Fish speciality night is Thursday, a chance to try oysters and lesser known varieties of fish. The building is over 600 years old - not immediately evident from the outside, but inside is rich with heavy timbers and open fires, and includes a separate dining area, ideal for parties of up to 30. The atmosphere is hospitable, the staff friendly and courteous.

What kind of cobs are "bread" here?

THE ALMA ARMS
Horseman Side, Navestock Side, Brentwood. Tel. (01277) 372629

Location: take Coxtie Green Road off A128 for 2 miles, right at T-junction, then right into Dytchleys Lane, left at end of lane - pub is 250 yds on right.
Credit cards: not accepted.
Bitters: Greene King Abbot, Rayments, Ridleys ESX.
Lagers: Kronenbourg, Fosters, Carlsberg.

Examples of bar meals (12 - 2:30pm, 7.00 - 9:30pm): *speciality homemade pies (eg steak, salmon & broccoli, chicken & mushroom, steak & stilton, Suffolk pie; steak & ale pie); home-made pasta & vegetarian dishes; mixed grill; fresh daily fish (eg salmon, trout); grills & steaks (incl. rump & T-bone); minted lamb; turkey steaks. Homemade desserts (eg cheesecake, sherry trifle, fruit crumbles, bread & butter pudding). Daily 3 course meal £6.45 (Sat. evening menu £8.95) Trad. Sun. roasts (incl. dessert) £6.75.*

NB: open for home-cooked meals all day until 9:30pm daily inc. Sundays.

Once off the main road the drive through the wooded and rolling Essex countryside is very pleasant, though not straightforward. So given that there can be very little passing trade, it speaks volumes that Alan and Jane Speight have run this busy rural inn for over 26 years. They have flourished through value, freshness and home cooking, complemented by a good range of ales and vast selection of wines. The inn was built in 1731 but only bore the 'Alma' title since the Crimean War battle of that name. The attractive bars are oak-beamed - the bar itself being brick with timber reliefs, the theme continued to the fireplaces. A new addition is the very pleasant 40-seater Victorian conservatory where persons over 14 years old may dine, but for really warm days there is a patio to the front. Rated by several national guides. Large car park.

ESSEX *By what name is the resident spook affectionately known?* INNS & PUBS

THE BEAR INN
The Square, Stock, nr Ingatestone. Tel: (01277) 840232

Location: just off Stock Street (B1007).
Credit cards: Mastercard, Visa, Delta, Switch.
Bitters: Friary Meux, Young's PA, Tetley, Calder's Cream, fortnightly guest.
Lagers: Castlemaine, Carlsberg.

Examples of bar/restaurant meals (lunch & evening, 7 days): *home-made chicken liver & whisky paté; breast of guinea fowl with warm salad; butterfly king prawns with cream & garlic; garlic ciabata; steamed garlic mussels in cream sauce; pot-roast shank of lamb in honey, mint & rosemary sauce; steak & ale pie; steaks; pan-fried skate wing in beurre noisette; coddled sea bass in soft herb crust; mushroom stroganoff ("to kill for!"); sweet & sour vegetable stir-fry; sandwiches; ploughman's; daily specials. Home-made desserts. Trad. Sun. roasts. "Will cook anything with 24 hrs notice."*

One of the region's best known pubs, The Bear traces its roots to Hereward the Wake. It was built by one of his descendants in the 15th century, and was named in honour of the great white bear - "the old man in the fur coat" - which he slew as a young man to win his spurs. With characteristic low ceilings, exposed timbers and open fires, the bars and dining room are cosy and warm - especially so for one customer of yore who, it is said, remains lodged in a chimney! Enthusiastic staff organise live music every other Sunday, plus monthly theme nights and charity events. Children have their own room, plus a games shed in the garden in summer. The function room, used by local societies, is available for buffets and private functions for up to 50 people.

From which house does some of the benching come?

THE ANCHOR INN
High Street, Canewdon, nr Rochford. Tel: (01702) 258213

Location: village centre.
Credit cards: Mastercard, Visa.
Bitters: Flowers IPA, Greene King IPA, Tetley.
Lagers: Castlemaine, Stella Artois, Carlsberg.

Examples of bar/restaurant meals (lunch & evening, 7 days): *Malaysian chicken; mushrooms en croute; Alabama chicken breast (coated in ground peanuts); medallions of pork with sweet & sour sauce; steaks & grills; 'snake & pigmy' pie; poachers pie; home-made lasagne; courgette & chilli bake; veg. curry; whole lemon sole; grilled salmon with hollandaise sauce; jacket potatoes; ploughman's; salads; rolls & sandwiches; daily specials eg tuna & pasta bake, breaded lemon sole stuffed with mushrooms in white wine sauce, steak & ale pie, steak & stilton parcel. Home-made fruit pies; bread & butter pudding with real ale; Yankie cherry waffle; speciality ice creams. Children's menu. Trad. Sun. roasts.*

On a bleak, misty winter's day you could still believe in witches in this eerily quiet part of Essex near the River Crouch, only minutes away from the bright lights of Southend. In the 17th century this would have been no joke, for Canewdon was at the centre of "Witches' Country", and many a poor soul met a grisly end at the stake, including Sarah, who is said to live on here in spirit. If so she has chosen well, for this 400-year-old inn is warm and accommodating, with a good name for cooking. Landlord (since 1994) Keith White welcomes families; there's a children's room and the garden has pets. Other diversions are a circular revolving pool table and Quiz Nights on the first Tuesday of each month. Combine your visit with a look at the local church and its stocks.

THE RED LION
The Street, Kirby-le-Soken, nr Frinton. Tel: (01255) 674832, Fax: (01255) 675110

Location: village centre, opposite church.
Credit cards: Mastercard, Visa, Delta, Switch.
Bitters: Adnams, Morlands Old Speckled Hen, Marstons Pedigree, Websters.
Lagers: Carlsberg, Fosters, Holsten, Kronenbourg.

Examples of bar meals (lunch & evening, 7 days): *home-made steak or chicken pie; steaks & grills; balti dishes; fresh whole plaice; scampi; salads; sandwiches; ploughman's; selection of vegetarian dishes; daily specials eg seafood gratin, chicken in port wine, loin of pork with honey & mustard. Chocolate trufito; spotted dick; apple pie; raspberry pavlova; gateau of the day.*

Examples of restaurant meals (as above): *breast of chicken with champagne & cream; halibut steak with lemon & herb butter; pork fillet with Calvados; Dover sole. Trad. Sun. roasts.*

Once past the infamous level crossing, escapees from publess Frinton have only a two-mile dash across open country to this much esteemed and well run 14th-century (1361, to be exact) hostelry - smugglers actually tunnelled their way here! One or two may linger yet, for it is reputedly haunted. Oak-beamed and warmed by open fires, its period atmosphere is very evident. Theme Nights afford an opportunity to dabble in the world's cuisines, but there's always a good choice of home-cooked food. Children are welcome and have a play area in the garden. Restaurant doubles as function room. Ample parking.

THE CRICKETERS
The Green, Sarratt. Tel: (01923) 263729

Location: on village green, 2 miles off jncn 18 of M25.
Credit cards: Mastercard, Visa, Amex.
Bitters: Courage, guest.
Lagers: Fosters, Kronenbourg.

Examples of bar/restaurant meals (lunch & evening, 7 days): *smoked fish terrine on dill & cucumber sauce; tomato & orange soup; hotpot of pheasant, quail & venison; chicken supreme with ginger, coriander & white wine sauce; breast of lamb with mustard & herb crust; many fish specials eg lime-marinated brill with avocado & red onion salsa; salads; jacket potatoes. Sweet cider pineapple fritters with coconut ice cream & hot chocolate sauce; rice pudding & fresh strawberry coulis. Trad. Sun. roasts (plus late afternoon sitting).*

NB: open all day - some cold food always available.

At the western extremity of the region, this lovely village is made very accessible by the M25. Yet it remains blissfully rural and unspoilt, just far enough away from the rumble of traffic, and with some fine country and riverside walks. Built around 350 years ago as three cottages, The Cricketers is now blessed with a roomy and stylish new restaurant extension; French doors lead to terrace and garden. With one or two necessary exceptions, all food (incl. desserts) is fresh and prepared on the premises by chef Martin Amos. His many interesting daily specials reveal his versatility, but seafood is clearly a particular strength. Barbecues are held in summer, there are monthly quiz nights and a dart board. Children welcome. Facilities for disabled and baby-changing.

HERTFORDSHIRE *Why was Christmas ruined in 1922?* INNS & PUBS

THE BRICKLAYER'S ARMS
Hogpits Bottom, Flaundon. Tel: (01442) 833322

Location: 5 mins from Bovingdon (nr Hemel Hempstead); from the south, go thro' village, left at X-roads, right at next X-roads.
Credit cards: Mastercard, Visa, Delta, Switch, Amex, Diners.
Bitters: Marston's Pedigree, Brakspears, 5/6 guests.
Lagers: Boddington Gold, Stella Artois, Heineken.

Examples of bar/restaurant meals (lunch & evening, 7 days): *home-made game paté; seafood platter (noted); ragout of lobster; Cajun red snapper; duck morello; broccoli & walnut bake; steaks & grills; steak & kidney pudding; trawlerman's pie; huge combo; fajitas; local sausages; ploughman's; sandwiches; blackboard specials eg thin strips of venison marinated in passion fruit & kiwi (served with rice rosti & kiwi coulis), artichoke bottoms filled with duxelle, prime Scotch fillet rolled in oats (pan-fried & finished with whisky sauce). Home-made bread & butter pudding; fruit crumbles; apricot & honeycombe bomb. Trad. Sun. roasts.*

Alpine by East Anglian standards, the Chilterns is a lovely area to explore, made very accessible by the M25. One of the joys of the peaceful leafy lanes is chancing upon a marvellous old country pub such as this, highly rated by major national guides for both food and beer. The menus are mouthwatering - staple pub favourites vie with the exotic (plus theme evenings, such as Chinese, Italian or round-the-world). Also uncommon is the service: orders are taken from table, not at the bar - licencees David and Sue Winteridge worked in hotels for years before coming here in April '96. Children are welcome and the large garden has 100 seats; live jazz is performed there on three Sundays every August. Whipsnade and St Albans only 20 mins.

THE GRAND JUNCTION ARMS
Bulbourne Road, Bulbourne, nr Tring. Tel & Fax: (01442) 890677

Location: by Grand Union Canal on main road through village.
Credit cards: Mastercard, Visa, Diners, Delta, Switch.
Bitters: Greenalls, Adnams, guest; plus dark mild.
Lagers: Carling, Stella Artois.

Examples of bar meals (lunch & evening except Mon evenings): *Highland whisky fondue; Scrumpy Jack chicken; Irish whisky pork; drunken ribs; Bulbourne omelette; home-made soups; steak & kidney pie; bangers & mash; lock-keeper's lunch; 'canal loaf'; chilli; rarebit; potato boats; mushroom, pepper & coconut curry; fresh onion 'blossom' (deep-fried with blue cheese dip - speciality); blackboard specials eg cheese & mushroom bake, home-made vegetable pie. Boatman's tart; apple kebabs with toffee sauce; apricot frangipan; chocolate sponge with chocolate sauce. Trad. Sun. roasts. Afternoon teas. Breakfasts on request.*

"Innkeeper of the Year" (London & Home Counties) from the British Institute of Innkeeping is a prestigious accolade; after just three years here Jackie and David Atkins can take pride in having won it. The garden of their 19th-century bargee's inn sweeps right down to the water's edge, and one can hire boats in summer - food and drink supplied! A small shop sells canal souvenirs. Other diversions are bar billiards, a shelf full of books, Sausage Nights (15 kinds), Quiz Night on Wednesdays, and every Sunday is Music Night - bring your own instrument (and there's no juke box or piped music!). Children will be amused by the budgies and a climbing frame. And naturally food is home-cooked and highly original.

HERTFORDSHIRE   *How many gentlemen are in waiting*   INNS & PUBS
              in the breakfast room?

THE RED LION
Kings Walden Road, Gt Offley, nr Hitchin. Tel: (01462) 768281

Location: off A505; left at top of hill into High Street, straight on for 600 yards.
Credit cards: Mastercard, Visa, Diners.
Accommodation: 5 dbls/twins; all en-suite, TV, tea & coff; hair- dryer & laundry service; £39.50 per room excl. breakfast.
Bitters: Timothy Taylor's Landlord, Boddington, Fuller's London Pride, Ruddles County, guest.
Lagers: Stella Artois, Heineken, Carling.

Examples of bar/restaurant meals (lunch & evening, 7 days, but bar snacks only Mon. evenings): *breaded mushrooms; deep-fried whitebait; chicken satay;16oz T-bone steak; chicken & smoky ham crumble; lemon & pepper haddock; sizzling cajun chicken; baltis; lasagne verdi; Texas beef hotpot; daily specials eg home-made steak & kidney pie; chilli; stroganoff; kangaroo steaks; salmon in bechamel sauce. Home-made apple pie; fruit crumbles; treacle sponge; toffee & apple cheesecake. Trad. Sun. roasts.*

If you have ever flown from Luton you probably know how scandalously expensive overnight accommodation is there, so it is a revelation to find this attractive 16th-century inn in a quiet, pleasant village just seven minutes' drive from the airport, offering comfortable bedrooms at such a reasonable rate. Even if you are staying firmly on the ground, the good home-cooked food and friendly family atmosphere make it well worth seeking out. New licensees (since April '96) Richard and Karen have made a number of changes - monthly live music, theme nights eg Curry, Pasta, Italian - and also plan children's play facilities in the sheltered garden. But unchanging are the ancient timbers, large inglenook and cottagey restaurant with open fire.

INNS & PUBS　　*Why do customers always get high here?*　　HERTFORDSHIRE

THE WHITE HORSE
Burnham Green, nr Welwyn. Tel: (01438) 798416

Location: on village green, one mile from Tewin.
Credit cards: Mastercard, Visa, Amex, Delta, Switch.
Bitters: Greene King IPA, Adnams, Burtons, Tetley, Caffreys, 2 guests.
Lagers: Lowenbrau, Carlsberg Pilsner & Export, Castlemaine, Carling Premier.

Examples from lunch menu (available every day, plus up to 8pm in bar): *filled jacket potatoes; sandwiches; fresh battered cod; local sausages; steaks; lasagnes; daily specials eg home-made pies, smoked haddock florentine, skate wing in black pepper butter; liver & bacon in rich onion gravy; pan-fried turkey escalope. Exceptional choice of home-made sweets eg chocolate, raspberry & hazelnut meringue; treacle & almond tart; fruit crumble; steamed sponge pudding. Trad. Sunday roasts.*

Examples from evening menu (daily): *coquilles St Jacques; moules mariniere; home-made patés & soups. Beef Wellington; salmon en croute; noisette of lamb with rosemary crust; blackboard specials.*

If you need reminding of what an agreeable county Hertfordshire can be, then a drive out to this idyllic 18th-century country pub is to be recommended. Warm and inviting, its timbered interior is on three levels, with a particularly attractive gallery upstairs. The dining area overlooks a large landscaped garden with duck pond, and there's also a heated patio area. Licencees Richard Blackett and Nicky Hill uphold high standards of cuisine coupled with friendly and efficient service. The restaurant has a no-smoking area, and well-behaved children are welcome at lunchtime and early evening.

HERTFORDSHIRE *Who's the cigar-smoking hustler at the bar?* INNS & PUBS

THE PLUME OF FEATHERS
Upper Green, Tewin. Tel: (01438) 717265

Location: edge of village, towards Burnham Green.
Credit cards: Mastercard, Visa, Mastercard, Switch, Eurocard.
Bitters: Adnams, Marston's Pedigree, Bass, Caffreys, 5 guests.
Lagers: Stella Artois, Carling.

Examples of bar meals (lunch & evening, 7 days): *Thai seafood curry; fresh fish of the day; steak & kidney pudding; pork & leek sausages; tomato, pepper & pesto tart; daily specials eg sizzling duck. Amaretto parfait; home-made pear & almond vanilla icecream; chocolate mousse cake.*

Examples of restaurant meals (as above): *crispy duck; Covent Garden terrine; fresh calamari & octopus. Steaks; fillet of red mullet with slithered almonds & king prawns; pot-roasted local rabbit; venison sausages with juniper berries & apple; baked field mushrooms with fresh corn & diced peppers in pepper sauce. Trad. Sun. roasts.*

Four chefs use only fresh produce (incl. pasta) and a lot of verve to make this 16th-century alehouse (sister pub to The Bricklayers at Flaundon) one of the area's best loved places to eat. Being in a very select neighbourhood, you may also find yourself rubbing shoulders with 'celebs'. There was none bigger than QE I, who used it as a hunting lodge. A skilled refurbishment has restored many period features, but perhaps most unusual is the gallery, an opulent sitting room with Persian rug. The very attractive restaurant overlooks a two-acre garden (with sandpit, volleyball, boules and barbecue), which itself commands wonderful views over farmland - a great venue for a wedding reception (marquee available). Toilets for disabled; baby-changing facilities.

THE FIVE HORSESHOES
FREEHOUSE & RESTAURANT
1 Church Road, Little Berkhamsted, nr Hertford.
Tel: Cuffley (01707) 875055, Fax: (01707) 876315

Location: village centre, opp. cricket ground (not to be confused with Berkhamsted, some 30 miles away).
Credit cards: Mastercard, Visa, Amex.
Bitters: Greene King Abbot, Ansells, McMullens, Theakstons.
Lagers: Kronenbourg, Labatts, Castlemaine.

Examples of bar meals (lunch & evening, 7 days): *grilled sardines in garlic butter; pork spare ribs with oriental sauces; vegetable curry; steak in ale pie; chilli; lasagne; sausage & mash; braised liver & bacon; best Scottish steak; chicken chasseur; stuffed belly of pork; roasts; salads; sandwiches; jacket potatoes; vegetarian dishes. Apple crumble; spotted dick; banana & rum cheesecake.*

Examples of restaurant meals (lunch & evening, 7 days, but occasionally closed Mons): *spiced soft roes on toast; stilton field mushrooms with herb crust & tomato sauce. Dover sole; sea bass with rosemary & garlic; lamb loin with onion & garlic in puff pastry; half roast duckling with apple sauce; fabulous Scottish steaks; vegetarian dishes. 10% service charge.*

Few other pubs or restaurants have their own butchery. Taste the beef here and you will know the difference: it cuts like butter. Everything is home-prepared and fresh; meat is bought direct from the farm, fish daily from the market. It is this attention to quality which has given Ray Curson 10 successful years at this 17th-century Grade II listed freehouse in one of Hertfordshire's most delightful villages. He also refurbished extensively, creating the fine galleried restaurant (available for private functions). Smart dress is appropriate here, but the characterful bars are quite informal. St George's Day, Burns Night and other special dates are always celebrated, and barbecues are held in the garden, weather permitting. Good wine list includes local Howe Green vineyard. Ample parking. Customer mailing list.

HERTFORDSHIRE *What unusual facility is generously offered by The Grand Hotel, Cairo?*

INNS & PUBS

THE SOW & PIGS
Cambridge Road, Thundridge, nr Ware. Tel: (01920) 463281

Location: on west side of A10, 3 miles north of Ware.
Credit cards: Mastercard, Visa, Switch.
Bitters: Adnams, Shipstones, Wadworth 6X, Tetley.
Lagers: Labatts, Stella Artois, Carling.

Examples of bar meals (lunch & evening, 7 days): *home-made soup; mushrooms in cider & stilton sauce; melon fan & grenadine syrup; steak; duck breast in passion fruit & orange sauce; pork fillet in apple cream sauce; special grill; whole grilled plaice; mushroom & courgette stroganoff; sandwiches; ploughmans; daily specials eg vegetable balti, ham & mushroom pie, pork chop with mustard sauce, Yorkshire fish & chips & mushy peas. Trad. Sun. roasts.*

You won't feel like a stranger for long here; the staff are notably welcoming and proprietor (since June '95) Meriel Riches (formerly of next-door Hanbury Manor) is rarely to be seen on the 'business' side of the bar, preferring to rub shoulders with customers. If it's no surprise to find pig collections displayed everywhere, then the diversity of the many pieces certainly is. Apparently the name derives from a card game popular when the inn was built in 1592 to serve passing coaches. Pig roasts are a succulent Bank Holiday treat, but the standard of food is always high, recognised by major national guides. There is a separate dining room but a marquee available for hire in the garden serves for functions, wedding receptions etc. Activity box for children. No indoor games or piped music.

THE BULL
113 High Street, Watton-at-Stone. Tel: (01920) 831032

Location: on main road through village.
Credit cards: Mastercard, Visa, Amex.
Bitters: Greene King, McMullens, Burton, Tetley.
Lagers: Carlsberg, Castlemaine.

Examples of bar/restaurant meals (lunch & evening, 7 days): *spicy potato wedges with barbecue sauce; prawn & pineapple brochette; chicken satay; chicken balti; chicken tikka masala; curry; chilli; barbecue spare ribs; steaks & grills; tuna & pasta florentine; liver & bacon; beef stroganoff; crispy veg. parcels; mushroom balti with naan; baguettes; ploughman's; sandwiches; daily specials eg salmon with cheese & herb sauce, grilled plaice. Rhubarb crumble; mincemeat bakewell; profiteroles; treacle sponge; spotted dick; toffee apple & pecan pie. Children's menu. Trad. Sun. roasts.*

The magnificent fireplace, lit in winter, is the first feature to catch the eye, but it is what is on the blackboard which makes this 15th-century coaching inn especially noteworthy and popular. It lists a wide diversity of choice, freshly home-made, with Indian dishes well represented as well as time-honoured English favourites. Look out for special evenings (usually Mondays), when the theme might be Curry, Italian or Chinese cooking, for example. Tuesday evenings see the large, characterful bar become the stage for live music. Experienced proprietors Mike and Bev Morris welcome children and have a play area, menagerie and barbecue in the garden. Large car park. Knebworth and Hatfield Houses not far.

THE GEORGE & DRAGON
High Street, Watton-at-Stone. Tel: (01920) 830285

Location: village centre, between Stevenage & Hertford.
Credit cards: Mastercard, Visa, Diners, Amex.
Bitters: Greene King. Plus Guinness & Murphy's stout.
Lagers: Harp, Kronenbourg, Stella Artois.

Examples of bar/restaurant meals (lunch & evening, except Sun. evening): *salad of sliced tomato, onions & fresh basil with prawns; smoked salmon & mackerel roulade with yoghurt, chive & caper dressing; chef's chicken Kiev; aubergine & goats' cheese baked gateau on piquant mix of red wine, leeks & mushrooms; millionaire's/billionaire's bun; fishcakes with yoghurt, cucumber & dill dip; savoury pancake filled with spinach, wild mushrooms & smoked ham; salads; sandwiches; chalkboard specials which nearly always include fresh fish. Home-made puddings.*

"The pub with the club atmosphere" is a fair description. Built as a pub in 1603, it exudes an air of comfort and well being, with its old beams, antique furniture and prints, and fresh flowers in abundance. To relax by the log fire with the papers (provided) and good food and drink is a simple but profound pleasure. But it is not only the warm hospitality which has secured a regular place - indeed a star rating - in the national guides; as a glance over the examples above will suggest, the cooking is of a high order and uncommonly original. Occasional special nights add further interest and the wine list is always excellent. Children welcome as far as facilities will allow, but there is a newly extended garden and patio. Ample parking.

What type of bushes are found in the Ale Bar? **HERTFORDSHIRE**

THE TILBURY (INN OFF THE GREEN)
Watton Road, Datchworth. Tel: (01438) 812496

Location: village centre, at crossroads.
Credit cards: Mastercard, Visa, Diners, Amex, Switch, Delta.
Bitters: Five-hides (own brew), Bass, Caffreys, guests.
Lagers: Warsteiner, Tennents, Staropramen.

Examples of bar/dining room meals (lunch & evening Mon - Sat, plus ALL DAY SUNDAY): *oriental fish saté; home-made beef & ale pie; beef & venison pie; lasagne; chicken balti; prawn & veg. balti; chicken tobago; lamb rosemary; steaks & grills; salmon in mushroom & white wine sauce; fresh trout with prawns & garlic butter; battered cod; vegetable curry; vegetable chilli; nut roast; vegetarian sausage; potato shells; sandwiches; ploughman's. Home-made bread & butter pudding; fruit crumble; treacle roly poly. Trad. Sun. roasts.*

Ian and Sheila Miller's superb (and moderately priced) own-brew beer would be reason enough for a visit, but tee-totallers will also be rewarded by the home-cooking, on a menu chalked daily on blackboards, and vegetarians well looked after. On top of that, it's also a fine building, dating from the 16th century, with cosy alcoves and a magnificent fireplace in the dining room. The Ale Bar (with dartboard) is quite unique, having stripped wood floor, exposed brickwork and tables made from barrels. It is here that 'fun-ghost' Algenon manifested himself as a green haze, and he also likes to play tricks in the kitchen. Perhaps he likes the monthly music nights on Thursdays. Children are welcome and the garden has an aviary. Knebworth and Hatfield Houses nearby.

HERTFORDSHIRE *What spirit might you find in the cellar?* INNS & PUBS

THE ROSE & CROWN
69 High Street, Ashwell, nr Baldock. Tel: (01462) 742420

Location: village centre.
Credit cards: Visa, Mastercard, Eurocard, Switch.
Bitters: Greene King.
Lagers: Harp, Kronenbourg.

Examples from lunch menu (not Mondays, except Bank Hols): *home-made lasagne; baked fillet of cod with prawns & cream; pasta Florentine; omelettes; baguettes; jacket potatoes; fresh fish & chip specials Tues & Thurs; daily specials eg boar & apple sausages, chilli. Ginger sponge with lemon sauce; summer pudding; chocolate pudding; treacle tart. Trad. Sun. roasts.*

Examples from evening menu (as above): *Toulouse sausages with fruit sauce; deep-fried potato skins with blue cheese; crispy prawn parcels with tomato & garlic; steak & onion pudding; chicken, ham & leek pudding; pigeon breast sautéd in rich fruit compote; pheasant supreme with duxelle stuffing; steaks; steamed sea bass with ginger & fresh lime; seafood au gratin; Tuscan bean garlic crostini.*

A regular in national good pub guides, this 15th-century coaching inn could nevertheless not be described as a 'foodie' pub. The menus are exceptionally tempting, but you are just as welcome if you are simply looking for a quiet, unhurried pint and good conversation in a convivial atmosphere. The bar is divided into four cosy areas, one set aside for games and another with a magnificent inglenook fireplace. But it is the 'nooky seat' which is seemingly most popular with courting couples. Children are welcome in eating areas and the very well kept garden to the rear of the car park. Ashwell is one of Hertfordshire's more picturesque villages.

INNS & PUBS *How many horns hang over the fireplace?* BEDFORDSHIRE

THE CHEQUERS
Queen Street, Stotfold. Tel: (01462) 730495

Location: east side of town; from by-pass, on to main street (old A507), first right.
Credit cards: Mastercard, Visa, Diners, Amex.
Bitters: Greene King, Rayments, occasional guest.
Lagers: Harp, Kronenbourg, Stella Artois.

Examples of bar/restaurant meals (available ALL DAY & EVERY DAY): *home-made chicken liver paté; mozarella melt; large leg of roast lamb in mint sauce gravy; char-grilled steaks; pork fillet in cherry sauce; tournedos rossini; pan-fried cod in lemon butter; vegetarian selection; home-made pizzas (take away or delivery); fresh fish & chips (Fridays); sandwiches; baguettes; omelettes; ploughman's; daily specials eg home-made curries, steak & ale pie. Home-made passion by chocolate; lemon cheesequake; raspberry mould. Trad. Sun. roasts.*

Being open all day, every day, and just minutes' from the A1, this appealing 16th-century inn, tucked away in a residential street just off the main road, is a Godsend to the weary traveller, as well as an agreeable watering hole for those just seeking good, home-made food. Masterchef Douglas Bollen took over here with wife Paula only in June 1996, and has already effected a considerable transformation. The dining room (doubles for functions) is located in a new extension, beamed and chintzy, but food is also served in the old bar, with a real log fire in the large inglenook in winter. Fortnightly theme nights include Jazz, Italian, Curry etc. Darts, pool and crib are indoor amusements, and the garden has petanque and children's play area. Duxford and Knebworth are nearby.

THE TUDOR OAKS LODGE & RESTAURANT
Taylors Road, Astwick. Tel & Fax: (01462) 834133

Location: west side of A1; from the north take the Astwick exit and turn immediately left into narrow lane.
Credit cards: Mastercard, Visa, Amex, Diners.
Accommodation: 1 sngl (£36 incl., £30 at weekends), 8 dbls/twins (£45, £35 at weekends). All en suite, TV, phone, hair dryer, trouser press, mini bar; 1 with 4-poster & jacuzzi.
Bitters: Courage Directors, Fullers London Pride, Boddingtons, many unusual guests (300+ in '96).
Lagers: Stella Artois, Red Stripe. Plus real ciders & perry.

Examples of bar meals (lunch & evening, 7 days): *home-made curries: steak & kidney pie; chicken & ham pie; pork with apple in cider pie; steaks; omelettes; mushroom stroganoff; ploughman's; many daily specials eg toad-in-the-hole, whole grilled sea bass, trucker's breakfast, Chicago ribs.*

Examples of restaurant meals (as above): *steak Tudor Oaks (with light cream & prawn sauce); chicken Valdostana (breast with ham, cheese, mushroom & tomatoes); grilled Dover sole; trout amandine. Trad. Sun. roasts. Senior Citizens' lunches £2.75 Mon-Fri.*

Literally on the border with Herts, this 15th-century coaching inn, shamefully derelict until 1978, has been restored to former glory, retaining the original oak beams and hand-made red bricks. On the upper of the two-tier bar comfortable Chesterfields sit in front of a huge fireplace. Upstairs is the heavily timbered and cottagey restaurant. There's monthly live entertainment in the night club, and discos Thursday to Saturday evenings. The well equipped bedrooms are in chalets around a pretty courtyard. The chef patron's high standards - all food is fresh and prepared on the premises - continue to earn a place in leading national guides. Conferences and parties catered for.

INNS & PUBS   *What less happy role did The Black Horse once play?*   BEDFORDSHIRE

THE BLACK HORSE
Ireland, nr Shefford. Tel: (01462) 811398

Location: off A600, 1 mile from Shefford towards Bedford.
Credit cards: not accepted.
Bitters: Bass, Worthington, Shepherd Neame Spitfire.
Lagers: Carling, Tennents Extra.

Examples from lunch menu (daily except Mondays): *home-made steak & kidney pie; roast loin of lamb; liver & bacon; chicken fillet Frederick; Mexican cheese & pasta bake; scampi; plaice. Trad. Sun. roasts.*

Examples from evening menu (daily except Mondays): *pork steak Normand; entrecote steak brie; half crispy roast duck; supreme of chicken Caribbean; lamb steak Barnett; poached natural haddock; lobster thermidor; grilled skate. Fresh fish night on Thursdays.*

NB: check whether pub is open Mondays.

This is one Ireland you can reach without crossing the water (unless you count the River Ivel). The odd name is a corruption of the original 'Highland'. Built around 300 years ago in the heart of the Whitbread Estate, it stands on high ground in pleasant rolling countryside. Also elevated is the standard of food, further augmented on theme nights, such as Thai or Suckling Pig. As the photo shows, the display of hanging baskets is stunning. There's also a well kept garden with swings, but inside is very agreeable too: oak-beamed, with open fires and a separate dining room. Roy and Gordon, with wives Pam and Jean, have been the cordial hosts for over eight years. Pool table. Shuttleworth, Swiss Garden and Old Warden Aerodrome (airshows and veteran cars) all nearby.

BEDFORDSHIRE *Where can a serpent be found in Old Warden?* INNS & PUBS

THE HARE & HOUNDS
Old Warden, nr Bedford. Tel: (01767) 627225

Photo courtesy Dave Hillyard

Location: village high street, 5 mins from A1, west from Biggleswade, 15 mins from Bedford.
Credit cards: Mastercard, Visa, Switch, JCB.
Accommodation: in nearby guesthouse - arrange through pub.
Bitters: Adnams, Old Speckled Hen, Chas Wells Eagle, IPA, Bombardier, Fargo, Mansfield, Velvet, Tanglefoot.
Lagers: Red Stripe, McEwans.

Examples of bar meals (lunch & evening, 7 days; OPEN FOR FOOD EVERY DAY UP TO 11PM, but not always in the afternoon): *sesame prawn toasts with seafood dip; large French-style omelettes; steak & kidney pie; country pie; cod; scampi; lasagne; steaks; garlic & herb turkey; lime & ginger chicken; rosemary & garlic lamb; dijon pork; deep shortcrust savoury vegetable flan; daily specials eg lamb sabzi, turkey korma, pasta dishes, rich cheesy pudding. Chocolate challenge; fruit crumbles; syrup sponge; spotted dick; super ice creams; light bread & butter pudding. Traditional Sunday roasts (choice of 2 with fresh steamed veg.)*

Here is a village to dispel any notion that Bedfordshire has nothing worth turning off the A1 for; a 'stage-set' vision of thatched 18th-century cottages clustered in a fold in the rolling countryside. It is also home to one of the county's better pubs, under family ownership since spring 1995. With many years' experience garnered in Berkshire, their philosophy is that this is not a restaurant selling beer, but a pub selling food. The latter is home-cooked, always using fresh ingredients, and served in platefuls, but drinkers are always welcome; no more than half the tables may be reserved and the atmosphere is very informal throughout the four bars, each with a charm of its own (one celebrates the life of aviator Richard Shuttleworth - the famous Shuttleworth Collection and Swiss Gardens are very nearby). Sheltered courtyard in the large garden. Family room usually available.

How did drinkers help the war effort?

THE KING'S ARMS
London Road, Sandy. Tel: (01767) 680276

Location: just off A1 near Bickerdike's Garden Centre (easiest approached from north).
Credit cards: Mastercard, Visa, Switch, Amex.
Accommodation: 4 dbls/twins in chalets; all en-suite, TV, tea & coff; £30 per chalet, brkfst extra.
Bitters: Greene King, Rayments.
Lagers: Harp, Kronenbourg, Stell Artois.

Examples of bar meals (lunch & evening except Sun. evening): *home-made paté; beef casserole; home-made pie of the day; curry; steak; scampi; plaice; salads; ploughman's; sandwiches; jacket potatoes; daily specials eg beef korma, venison pie, Whitby haddies.*

Examples of restaurant meals (as above): *fillet stilton (speciality); pork Somerset; beef stroganoff; game pie; grilled Dover sole; fillet of salmon in asparagus sauce; venison steak with cranberry sauce; cashew nut balls; spinach & ricotta cheese cannelloni. Trad. Sun. roasts.*

The many admirers (including major national guides) of Ken and Jean Parry during their 13 years at The Mad Dog, Little Odell, should note that they are now resident proprietors of this warm, characterful and refurbished 17th-century coaching inn on the old Gt North Road. As ever, they offer "sustenance and shelter" to the weary traveller, in the form of a wide range of chef-prepared food, good wines and ales, and very affordable accommodation, well suited to business people or visitors to RSPB, Old Warden Aerodrome and Swiss Gardens. A small function room takes up to 14 people. Children are welcome in the dining room up to 8pm; the garden has a barbecue (occasional) and four petanque courts.

BEDFORDSHIRE *Who's the goose?* INNS & PUBS

THE BELL
Horsefair Lane, Odell. Tel: (01234) 720254

Location: village centre.
Credit cards: not accepted.
Bitters: Greene King.
Lagers: Harp, Kronenbourg, Stella Artois.

Examples of bar meals (lunch & evening, 7 days, except Sun. evenings in winter): *venison casserole; spicy chicken casserole; stilton, walnut & cream cheese pie; spinach, bacon & cream cheese roulade; creamy fish, mushroom & broccoli pie; shepherds pie; steak & kidney pie; turkey, leek & mushroom pie; chicken Kiev. Bakewell tart; boozy chocolate mousse; pecan nut pie; whisky ginger cream; pineapple raisin cheesecake.*

NB: open ALL DAY SAT. & SUN. in summer (food at normal hours).

It looks every inch the ideal thatched counry pub, and for once appearances are not deceiving. Tucked away in a quiet village not far from Odell Country Park, its 16th-century origins are apparent from the superb inglenook and exposed beams in the five rather cosy bar areas. One may eat anywhere (including the patio) and be sure of good, home-cooked food, prepared by the landlady herself, Doreen Scott. She and husband Derek have, over the past 11 years, earned the respect of the major national guides and local people, who appreciate the friendly atmosphere and absence of wailing juke-boxes etc. Children have an area set aside for them but will be sure to head for the little river which tumbles past the end of the garden (when not in drought!).

INNS & PUBS *Who was the author of the letter (dated 1794)* BEDFORDSHIRE
found in a window frame?

THE CROSS KEYS
High Street, Pulloxhill. Tel: (01525) 712442

Location: off A6 between Luton & Bedford.
Credit cards: Mastercard, Visa, Switch.
Bitters: Chas. Wells Fargo & Eagle, Adnams Broadside, Old Speckled Hen.
Lagers: McEwans, Red Stripe, Kellerbrau.

Examples of bar/restaurant meals (lunch & evening, 7 days): *fresh mushrooms in garlic butter; trout; steaks & grills; pork cordon bleu; lobster; roast duckling; salads; ploughman's; daily specials eg battered cod, hot & spicy pastie, deep-fried haddock in mornay sauce, duck in orange/cherry sauce. Home-made fruit pies; butterscotch ice cream with toffee chunks; Grandma's butter pecan. Trad. Sun. roasts.*

Acker Bilk, Kenny Baker, Charlie Galbraith and other famous jazz musicians enjoy playing here at the regular Sunday-night bash (entry free); like the customers, they appreciate the bonhomie and special atmosphere. This in part derives from the 15th-century building itself, but mostly it is due to the 26 years' stewardship of Peter and Sheila Meads and their long-serving staff. When they took over a pint of bitter was 71/2d (old pence), soup was 1/6 and a steak 12/6! Today's prices still afford excellent value, a temptation to eat out more often. The 80 wines listed (clarets a speciality) are also modestly priced, and there are occasional wine-tasting evenings with food to match. The attractive restaurant (available for functions) overlooks 10 acres of grounds - room enough for a marquee, barbecue, cricket pitch, boules, pitch and putt and caravan park! Three-course (+ coffee) senior citizens' lunch £4.50 Mon - Fri.

THE MAGPIES
Bedford Street, Woburn. Tel: (01525) 290219

Location: on main street, town centre.
Credit cards: not accepted.
Accommodation: 8 dbls/twins; 1 en suite, all with TV, tea & coff. From £25 - £45 per room.
Bitters: Marston's Pedigree, Ruddles.
Lagers: Carlsberg, Fosters, Holsten.

Examples from lunch menu (Mon - Sat, plus trad. Sun. roasts): *cannelloni stuffed with mushrooms & bacon; Mexican-style tacos; omelettes; jacket potatoes; BLT; filled French bread; daily specials eg curried pork, pasta tubes with spicy sausage.*

Examples from evening menu (Tues - Sat): *mixed pepper & cream cheese mousse with toasted ciabatta; warm chicken & leek tartlet; oriental noodle salad with prawns; boneless cod fillet with herb & lemon crust; grilled egg plant with sweet pepper & tomato mille-feuille; tender breast of chicken with dried tomato & shallot sauce; daily specials eg kangaroo, wild boar. Glazed apple sponge with lemon custard; dark chocolate cheesecake; strawberry shortbread.*

Even without the famous Abbey and Safari Park nearby, Woburn is one of England's premier villages, its dignified and historic main street well worth a long drive. Be sure to include this hospitable, timbered,16th-century coaching inn, restaurant-oriented but with a small, cosy bar, run personally by Sylvia and Len Beswick and family. Grandson-in-law Andrew is chef; he hails from down under, but his virtuosity extends well beyond the preparation of kangaroo! Value-for-money is also exceptional: Pasta Evenings on Tuesdays, for example, offer all you can eat for an amazing £3.95. Another favourite time to visit is at the Oyster Festival on the first Sunday of September - good idea to book a bedroom. Function room. Car park.

What is reality according to M. Mortimer Junior?

THE GLOBE INN
Globe Lane, off Stoke Road, Linslade. Tel: (01525) 373338, Fax: (01525) 850551

Location: off A416 Milton Keynes/Stoke Hammond road.
Credit cards: Mastercard, Visa, Diners, Amex.
Bitters: Tring, Marstons, Fuller's London Pride, Old Speckled Hen, guests.
Lagers: Becks, Kronenbourg, Fosters.

Examples of bar/dining room meals (lunch & evening, 7 days): *famous beef pie; sizzling steaks; fillet of pork with whisky & mushroom sauce; breast of duck with hot raspberry & whisky sauce; seafood & potato bake; salmon in leek & dill sauce; rack of lamb; bhalti; lasagne; vegetarian dish of the day; jacket potatoes; fresh rolls; daily specials eg seafood risotto, chicken breast in truffle sauce.* "Best dauphinoise potatoes in England." *Famous banoffee pie; bread & butter pudding; treacle sponge; cheesecake with raspberry coulis. Trad. Sun roasts.*

NB: advisable to book min. 2 weeks ahead for weekends.

Listen for the gasps of pleasant surprise as you round the bend on the long slope down to this early-19th-century canalside inn (national winner of 'Canals Alive' 1996). Bedecked with flowers and surrounded by country walks, it is one of the county's most inviting prospects. The rambling, timbered interior lives up to the promise; a glass of mulled wine by one of the three log fires makes winter seem quite bearable. Also radiating joviality are Clive and Tricia George and staff. Clive, who describes himself as a loud Welshman and fervent Man. Utd supporter, likes food and fun - don't miss his beerfest with live music and pig roast every August Bank Holiday. Food is taken seriously, though; its often "different" and always fresh - no chips or peas! Children are made welcome and have a play area in the garden. Tables and chairs on waterside patio. Small weddings etc catered for.

LOCATOR MAP

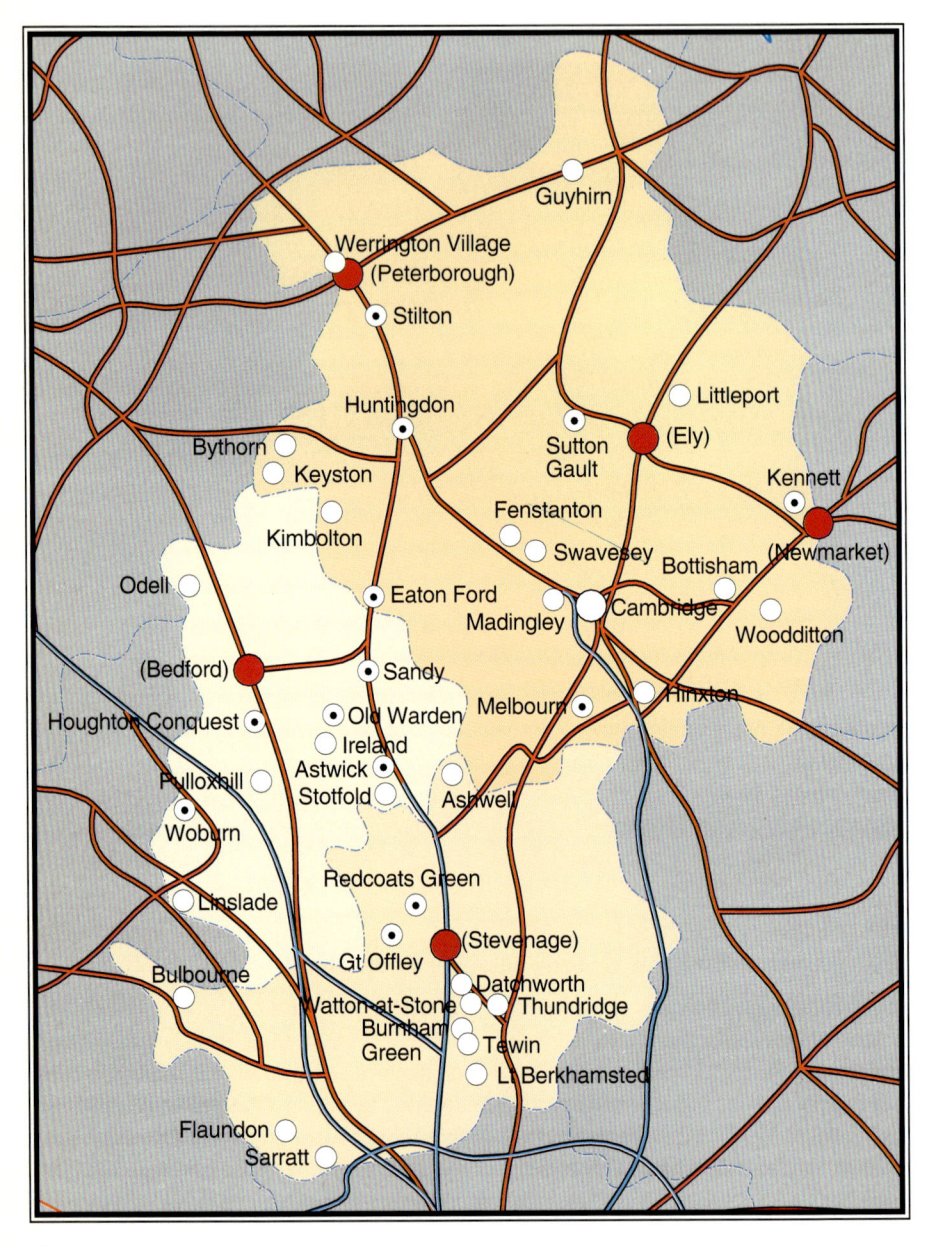

● Accommodation

186

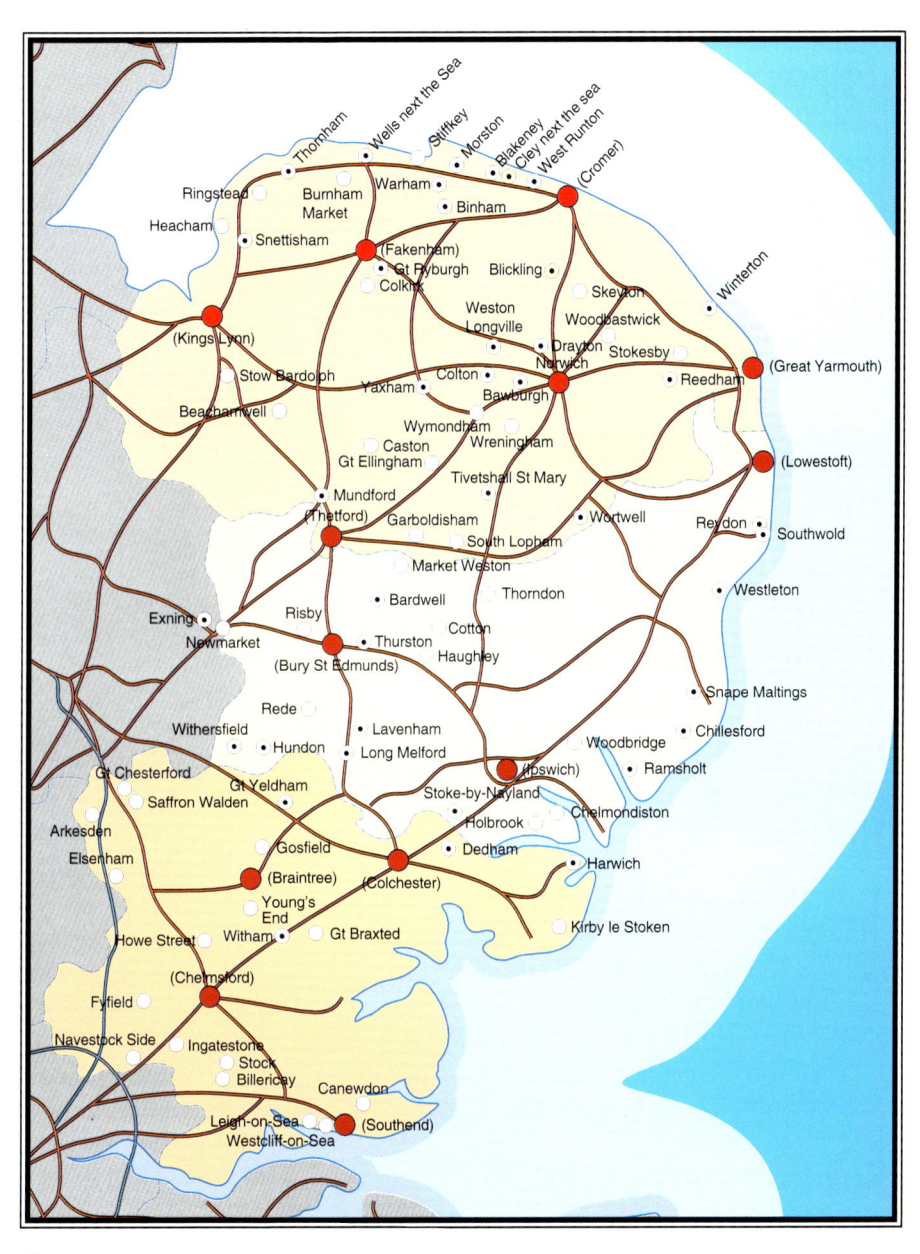

LOCATOR MAP

● Accommodation

INDEX

Bedfordshire

* Astwick, Tudor Oaks 178
* Houghton Conquest, Knife & Cleaver...91
   Ireland, Black Horse 179
   Linslade, Globe Inn 185
   Odell, Bell 182
* Old Warden, Hare & Hounds..180
   Pulloxhill, Cross Keys 183
* Sandy, King's Arms 181
   Stotfold, Chequers 177
* Woburn, Magpies..184

Cambridgeshire

   Bottisham, Stocks Restaurant 53
   Bythorn, Bennett's Restaurant at White Hart 63
   Midsummer House Restaurant 52
* Eaton Ford, Eaton Oak..147
   Fenstanton, King William IV 148
   Guyhirn, Oliver Twist 145
   Hinxton, Red Lion Freehouse 150
* Huntingdon, Old Bridge Hotel..67
   Keyston, Pheasant 65
   Kimbolton, New Sun Inn...146
   Littleport, Fen House Restaurant 57
   Madingley, Three Horseshoes 55
* Melbourn, Sheen Mill Hotel & Restaurant 69
* Stilton, Bell Inn Hotel & Restaurant 61
* Sutton Gault, Anchor 59
   Swavesey, Trinity Foot...149
   Werrington Village, Cherry House Restaurant 62
   Woodditton, Three Blackbirds 144

Essex

   Arkesden, Axe & Compasses 152
   Billericay, Duke of York...85
   Canewdon, Anchor Inn 163

* Accommodation

* Dedham, Le Talbooth 75
Elsenham, Crown 153
Fyfield, Black Bull 160
Gosfield, Green Man 156
Gosfield, King's Head 155
Gt Baddow, Russells Restaurant 79
Gt Braxted, Du Cane Arms 158
Gt Chesterford, Plough 151
* Gt Yeldham, Waggon & Horses 154
Gt Yeldham, White Hart 73
* Harwich, Pier Restaurant & Hotel 77
Howe Street, Green Man 159
Ingatestone, Little Hammonds 87
Kirby-le-Soken, Red Lion 164
Leigh-on-Sea, Edelweiss Swiss Restaurant 83
Navestock Side, Alma Arms 161
Saffron Walden, Old Hoops 71
Stock, Bear Inn 162
Westcliff-on-Sea, Alvaro's 81
* Witham, Crofters Restaurant 78
Young's End, Green Dragon 157

Hertfordshire

Ashwell, Rose & Crown 176
Bulbourne, Grand Junction Arms 167
Burnham Green, White Horse 169
Datchworth, The Tilbury (Inn off the Green) 175
Flaundon, Bricklayer's Arms 166
Gt Offley, Lobster Tail Restaurant 94
* Gt Offley, Red Lion 168
Lt Berkhamsted, Five Horseshoes 171
* Redcoats Green (nr Hitchin), Redcoats Farmhouse Hotel 93
Sarratt, Cricketers 165
Tewin, Plume of Feathers 170
Thundridge, Sow & Pigs 172
Watton-at-Stone, Bull 173
Watton-at-Stone, George & Dragon 174

* Accommodation

INDEX

Norfolk

* Bawburgh, King's Head 117
  Beachamwell, Gt Dane's Head..120
* Binham, Chequers Inn 105
* Blakeney, Kings Arms 107
* Blakeney, White Horse Hotel & Freehouse 106
* Blickling, Buckinghamshire Arms 111
  Burnham Market, Fishes' Restaurant 7
  Caston, Red Lion 19
* Cley-next-Sea, Three Swallows 108
  Colkirk, Crown 110
* Colton, Ugly Bug Inn..118
* Drayton, Stower Grange Restaurant with Rooms 28
  Garboldisham, Fox Inn 126
  Gt Ellingham, Crown Inn Freehouse & Restaurant 122
* Gt Ryburgh, Boar Inn 109
  Heacham, Ristorante La Villetta 6
* Morston, Morston Hall 11
* Mundford, Crown Hotel & Restaurant...121
  Norwich, Adlard's 27
  Norwich, Brasted's..25
* Reedham, Ferry Inn 116
  Ringstead, Gin Trap Inn 101
  Skeyton, Goat Inn 112
* Snettisham, Rose & Crown 100
  South Lopham, White Horse Inn 125
  Stiffkey, Red Lion 103
  Stokesby, Ferry Inn 114
  Stow Bardolph, Hare Arms 119
* Thornham, Lifeboat Inn...102
* Tivetshall St Mary, Old Ram 124
* Warham, Three Horseshoes 104
* Wells-next-the-Sea, Crown Hotel 9
* West Runton, Mirabelle 15
  West Runton, Pepperpot 13
* Weston Longville, Brasted's on the Park 23
* Winterton, Fisherman's Return 115
  Woodbastwick, Fur & Feather Inn 113

190   * Accommodation

* Wortwell, Dove Restaurant 29
　Wreningham, Bird in Hand 123
　Wymondham, Number 24 21
* Yaxham, Yaxham Mill Freehouse & Restaurant 17

Suffolk

* Bardwell, Six Bells Country Inn 47
　Chelmondiston, Butt & Oyster 136
* Chillesford, Froize Inn 134
　Cotton, Trowel & Hammer Inn 129
* Exning, Rosery Country House Hotel 51
　Haughley, Old Counting House Restaurant 45
　Holbrook, Compasses Inn 137
* Hundon (Brockley Green), Plough Inn 142
* Lavenham, Angel Hotel 140
* Long Melford, George & Dragon 139
　Long Melford, Scutchers Bistro 43
　Market Weston, Mill Inn 127
　Newmarket, Number 9 Restaurant 49
　Ramsholt, Ramsholt Arms 135
　Rede, Plough 141
* Reydon, Cricketers 31
　Risby, White Horse 128
* Snape Maltings, Plough & Sail 133
* Southwold, Crown Hotel 33
* Southwold, King's Head 131
* Southwold, Swan Hotel 34
* Stoke-by-Nayland, Angel Inn 138
　Thorndon, Black Horse Inn & Stables Restaurant 130
* Thurston, Thurston Grange Hotel & Restaurant 48
* Westleton, Crown 132
* Withersfield, White Horse Inn 143
　Woodbridge, Captain's Table Seafood Restaurant 41
　Woodbridge, Riverside Restaurant 39

* Accommodation

NOTES